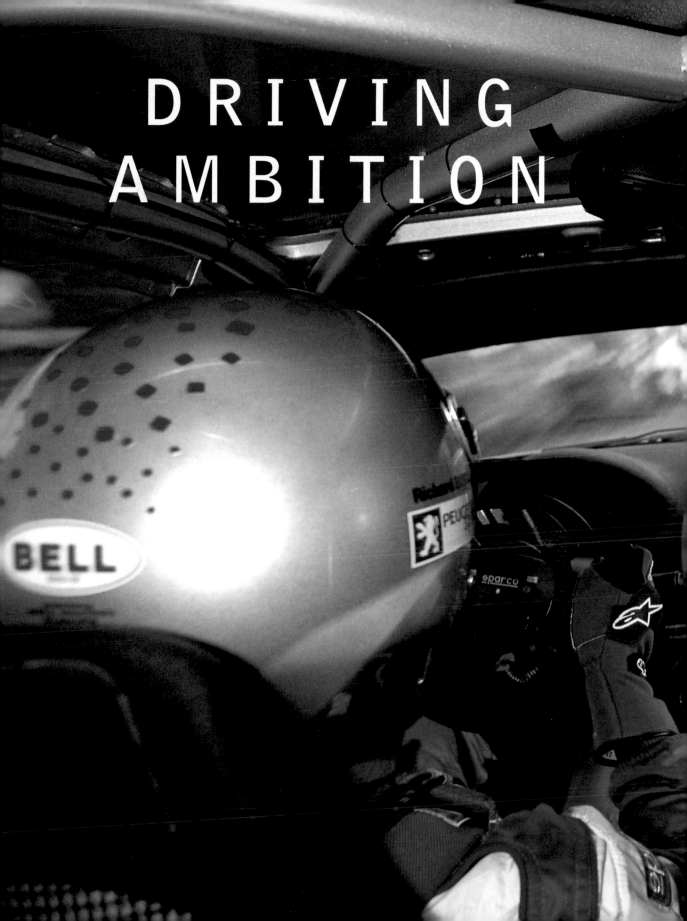

DRIVING
AMBITION

RICHARD
BURNS

DRIVING
AMBITION

Photography by
Peter Fox and McKlein

Hodder & Stoughton

Contents

For Dennis and Eileen Pettafor

What it's all about...

Driving a rally car is a drive like no other in a car like no other. We spend most of it at over 70 m.p.h., changing gear every two or three seconds. It's ferocious stuff. Afterwards you either smile, swear or are violently ill. But you won't forget it for the rest of your life.

Flat out in fifth: everything goes by so quickly but still I tell myself, 'keep your foot down'.

I'm off the start line and up to speed very quickly – through fourth gear, into fifth, 90 m.p.h. I check on the road condition. It's smooth here, double-width tarmac, maybe half the width of a racetrack.

To go faster than I should into the first corner I hook the inside wheels of my car over the edge of the road. I get to the apex and drop my wheels over the inside of the tarmac – it tugs the car on the inside front and rear wheels. If I get an early corner wrong I lose a lot of speed because I lose grip on the apex, come out too far sideways and I'm not on the power early enough.

There are blind sections of road here. I feel as if I can't get through. I'm doing 70 m.p.h., but I can only see 10 metres in front of me.

Suddenly the road surface changes from new tarmac to old, which gives more grip: it's bumpy but abrasive, made with slightly bigger stones. The new is smooth, very black. On smooth tarmac the car is just sliding, sliding, sliding. Sometimes I reach really black road – slippery tarmac that has melted in the sun. I keep clear of that.

Quickly through to the village – third gear, 60 m.p.h. corners. I don't see the buildings, just the road. According to my pace notes, the road is wider here but it's more difficult to drive: there's no definite edge. I adjust my line quickly if I see mud or a stone on the road. I mustn't let things happen too quickly.

The road takes me left, right, left, right again, out the other side of the village and down a hill to another corner. Hook it! Next a quick junction and then a junction left, all on old tarmac – there's a bank on the inside and a fence on the outside, with fence posts and wire in between. This is a switchback of quick corners – the car jumps, launching itself from one to another.

Up into fifth gear. Nearly the fastest stretch of the stage. I can keep the car straight for 70–80 metres. There are corners. I take them flat out in fifth gear. Now I'm travelling at 100 m.p.h. plus – easily! Again the road is blind.

Into the corner early – a fraction too much speed and I'm knackered.

I turn into the apex of the next corner. There's a slight camber on this bit of road. Good – I can go in quicker than I thought. The camber slopes down to the inside of the corner. I get good grip – it's like banking, small but effective. A junction right and I'm on a brilliant stretch – my favourite in this stage. It's much slower now. These are second- and third-gear corners – 30 m.p.h., maybe rising to 50 or 60. The road is flat, old, and at the side it rounds off, so again I can hook the inside of the corners. But there's no space between them. I have to tell myself to breathe. The road carries me into the first, on to another, down a bit – another, right this time, that one tightens and flicks me into the next. This is long, turning left; it tightens and tightens.

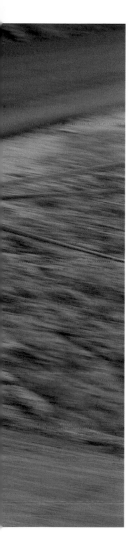

In a split second I realize that if I come in with a fraction too much speed at the entrance to the corner, I'm knackered. I go in early – I can't take a line because the car is moving still from the previous corner. I can't go wide for the next corner because the weight of the car, its momentum, has pushed me to the apex. I can't get on the power, I can't brake because the tyres are already at the limit of their grip. I have to rely on the car – whoa! The only thing slowing me down is the friction of the tyres laterally. At this point, I'm not really doing anything, just waiting until the end of the corner to get back on the power. Here, as quickly as my co-driver, Robert Reid, talks, something happens. He calls a corner – bang! I respond.

I do everything Robert tells me – he calls the corner – bang! I respond.

Corsica 2002 and no time to experience village life.

'Medium right, a K corner (a 45-degree angle), a K left, K left plus, then an easy right, 20 fast left, medium right minus, braking, 20 K right minus.' It happens as quickly as it is spoken.

Downhill now – a fantastic switchback, more quick stuff and much more blind road. Now, lots of long corners over long crests. I get them just right and I can feel it. I can probably only see five metres ahead because there are some fairly severe crests – up, down, up. Fantastic!

Up to a very tight hairpin right, and on to the length of road that takes you to the finish. It's double width, starts slowly, over a couple of bridges, in second gear, 35 m.p.h., really tight, good grippy Tarmac, but the tyres are going off.

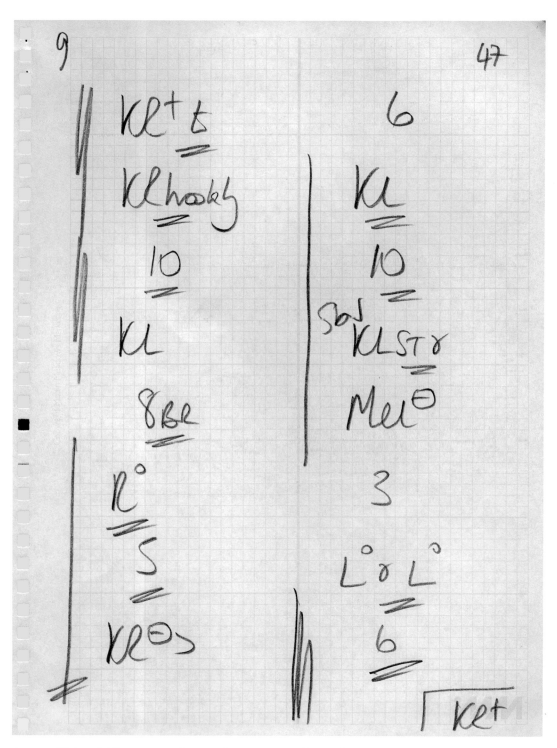

A page of Robert Reid's pace notes from Corsica 2002. Every driver and co-driver develop their own 'language' and this is ours. 'K' refers to the angle of the bend, the numbers are distances, 'BR' is brake – easy, really.

I have six kilometres of the stage left. There is a long climb uphill now, lots of long fourth-gear corners. I take these at maybe 80 m.p.h., and they push, because I can feel my tyres are already knackered.

The car slides out. I have to stay off the power until I feel the tyres coming back: if I turn in and slide the car all the way through the corner, I'll destroy them at the end. But I want to be on the power as much as I can because it's long and uphill. I see the section where lots of people come off – just before the end. There are lots of black tyremarks. From here on it's downhill to the finish and there are loads of cuts on the way down where I can put the whole car off the road if I want to.

But now the brakes are going off! There is one quick pitch up into fifth gear and still lots more corners to do – 70 metres then

a slight left. Another 70 metres, flat left this time – get the braking point exactly right here: I could lose time lifting too early or even go off completely.

In the last five kilometres I've got my foot on and off the gas every five seconds. Over the rest of it, I've been on and off every two or three seconds.

That's it – we're done. It's the end of the stage. I'm sweating but not out of breath. I feel warm, my hands are wet. My tyres are steaming, overheating: they're knackered. They're designed to go 56 kilometres – they've done 60. Over the last five or six they were ruined, especially that last slog with the full weight on the lateral grip of the car. They'll never be used again.

My office.

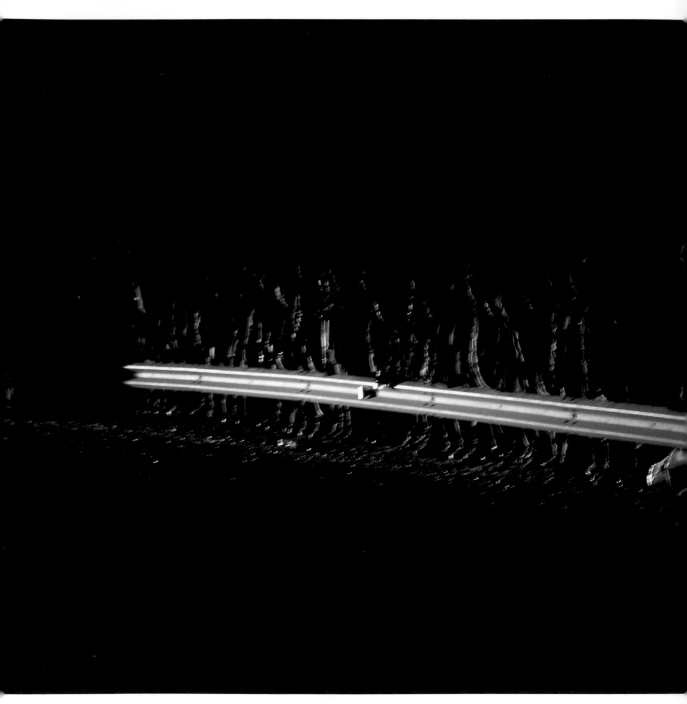

*Dedication: fans will stand and wait for hours just to see you smoke past them in a nanosecond.
This was taken during the Monte Carlo Rally in 2002.*

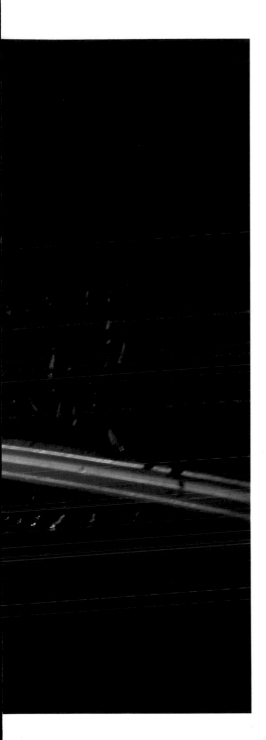

There's nothing in my life that takes over my mind as completely as driving at speed. What I have just tried to describe was the Lopigna stage on the Corsica rally. In 2002, in my new Peugeot 206 WRC, I recorded my first fastest stage on tarmac. It's one of my favourites in the Championship: it is 27.81 kilometres long and at an average speed of 92 k.p.h., took me 18 minutes, 11.6 seconds to drive. Fantastic

When I'm rallying I do everything my co-driver tells me to do from the notes I made in preparation. I must. Sometimes it feels as if I should lift my foot and slow down. But I keep it down and I'm glad I have. You lift when you're unsure – not confident, slow. There are times in a stage when I have to tell myself to breathe. I will have been holding my breath without realizing it.

In many ways rallying isn't like driving. It's about trying to get from the entry of a corner to the exit at the highest possible speed. Often that doesn't even involve steering. Instead I use the energy and momentum of the car. Whatever the speed, whatever the corner, the philosophy is still the same: get the car through the corner on the limit of the grip. There's no time to think about failure. Occasionally I notice what's going on outside the car but that's a distraction. Normally the only things going through my mind are the instructions coming from my co-driver.

The fastest I have ever been in a rally car is 239 k.p.h., which is 155 m.p.h. That was on the Safari Rally two years ago. I don't think I will ever go faster than that. It was downhill on a very smooth, straight piece of road and it took an age to slow the car down. I was virtually flying.

The car moves around all the time. In Africa I look forward to the end of the really high-speed stuff, and I sit there thinking, 'No other car is going faster than this. I know I'm taking time out of everybody else'. If I have an advantage I make as much use of it as I can.

New Zealand 1997.

Rally cars are smelly. They're full of bad air. It's the heat and the dust, and if you open the window you get, not petrol fumes, but a vapour smell. You know a new car: everything smells like it's burning, singeing, because everything is running in. I like the end of a wet stage in New Zealand or Great Britain when mud is caked over the car, particularly the disc brakes and the exhaust. You can smell the burning.

I hear three sounds in the car more than any other: the engine, the stones underneath it, and Robert's voice. Occasionally I hear things going on outside, like air-horns. I can hear the tyres on Tarmac if I've got it wrong and I'm going sideways in a Hollywood squeal.

When things are going well, I'm more relaxed. When things are tight, I have to make myself slow down because I know I'm overcompensating. It's important to slow my brain to a normal speed and try to relax. When I'm absolutely on it, the dashboard lights tell me when to change up but I always hang on for a few more revs. That noise gives me an extra sense of urgency, of speed, and makes me feel that I am going better.

I find myself smiling in the car sometimes, towards the end of a stage when I know I couldn't have driven it any better than I did. It's rare when that happens: you can't keep anything to yourself because everything you do is caught on one of the in-car TV cameras.

I like to sit low in the car, relatively straight-legged, but I like the wheel to be quite close to me. If that ratio isn't right I have trouble feeling the car. I feel what the car is doing with my fingertips and my backside. I have to have good contact. When you're braking you need to feel how much grip you've got. You get that feeling through the pedals and through the steering-wheel. When you're in a corner you feel the lateral grip through your backside and steering-wheel. If you start slipping at the rear you feel it through your backside; at the front, it's through the steering-wheel.

My gear shift is on the steering-wheel. I pull it to change up, push to change down. You use the clutch to start and stop but not at any other time. You brake with your left foot, accelerate with the right. All of the other key controls are on the dashboard.

You sweat a lot, even in the cold – like Sweden. On a normal day, I drink about 10 litres of water, roughly 20 pints. I have 'camel back' equipment in the car with pipes so I can drink while I'm driving the stages. Surprisingly, Safari, despite the temperatures, is not the hottest place to rally because the high speeds create air-flow through the car. The hottest, by far, is Cyprus. First, it is nearly 40°C outside, and second, the average speed is rarely more than 40 m.p.h (60 k.p.h.). In tests last year, the temperature climbed to 70°C in the Subaru.

I spend probably half of the time on a rally driving at over 70 m.p.h. In places in Kenya, I can even go without changing gear for a couple of kilometres. On a normal rally, though, I change gear every two or three seconds. Occasionally I use the handbrake to help me turn, maybe once or twice in a stage.

I have controls on the dashboard for brake balance, for the amount of tightness in the front, centre and rear differentials. You can adjust when and how much it locks, and how free it is when you're braking. It's infinitely variable. The diffs work all the time, limited with their slip capability 100 per cent. If you're on full power they're locked until you try to turn or brake. They stay locked when braking, but free up as you turn.

The brain in the car, the computer, controls the diffs, and you can program it around your braking, acceleration, steering or 'G' (gravitational pull), brake pressure, throttle or steering angle. I have my throttle pedal set quite short; probably the total travel is about two inches, if that, so it is quite sensitive. You can set it anywhere you like within the throttle range. This has been possible since electronic or 'fly-by-wire' throttles were introduced three years ago. The sensitivity is much finer than it is on a road car.

People have said that a drive in the car is ferocious and bruising, but you only get out bruised if you've had a crash. The co-driver might suffer a bit, but the driver is always tensed against the wheel and the pedals. The co-driver has only his footplate to steady himself, nothing for his upper body except his safety harness.

I know when I have made a good time – it's instinctive – but if someone has beaten it, I think, OK, fair play to them. Because I'm driving against the clock, I have only myself to blame for being slow. After all, I'm surrounded with things to help me: the best co-driver, the car set up to the best I can get it, and the best possible preparation with pace notes and testing.

Until they changed the rules for the 2002 season, rallying was a very tactical sport. The winner of each day started first the next day, which was a big disadvantage on gravel. You want to be driving when the surface has been 'swept' by other cars – a smooth surface equals a quick surface. So, unlike Formula One, it wasn't always best to be fastest. In Cyprus, Greece and New Zealand drivers used to hang back to try and lose time at the end of the last stage on days one and two. Crazy stuff. The best place to finish was between third and sixth, no more than a minute behind the leader. That way, someone else would go off first and 'sweep' the gravel off the stage. Now the leader of each day doesn't start first the following morning, so I reckon it's a much better test of the driver and the car.

By regulation, for safety reasons my Peugeot's engine is restricted to around 300 horsepower. An equivalent road Peugeot GTi is around 135–40. I can accelerate from 0 to 60 in about four seconds on tarmac. It deadens out at high speed because the engine power normally tails off. Remember, exceptionally high speeds aren't appropriate in rallying because the roads are never straight. The road-going GTi will do 0–60 in eight or

All done – for the time being. A moment to relax before the next stage.

nine seconds. The rally car halves that time: the whole point of the rally car is that it must accelerate as quickly as possible throughout the mid-range.

When I take someone out in the car, they swear and scream a lot. Occasionally they feel sick but generally I leave them with a big smile on their face. When I give people rides the mechanics love it: they've all been in the car and they know what it can do because they work on it, but they *still* can't believe it.

A ride in a rally car is a battering experience. You get used to it, but if you've been out of the car for two weeks then get back in you know about it. Even a single run leaves a normal person with an aching neck for a few days.

Who was sick in the car? Channel Four presenter, Jeremy Hart. But it was in exceptional circumstances. We were in Greece and it was 35°C outside and he was in full overalls. Also, you can't drive on a full stomach. I have breakfast every day and I have a bit of pasta the moment I get into each service area, so that it has gone down when I get back into the car. When you're on the stage your heart rate is anywhere between 150 and 180 beats per minute, which is what it would be if you were jogging or running, and you would never go jogging or running on a full stomach.

For some reason, though, no one told Jeremy.

The Greatest Day of My Life

I became World Rally Champion on Sunday, 25 November 2001. I finished third in the Rally of Great Britain, which gave me enough points to win the title. But the story of the greatest day of my life started on the previous Friday in a way I had never dared imagine . . .

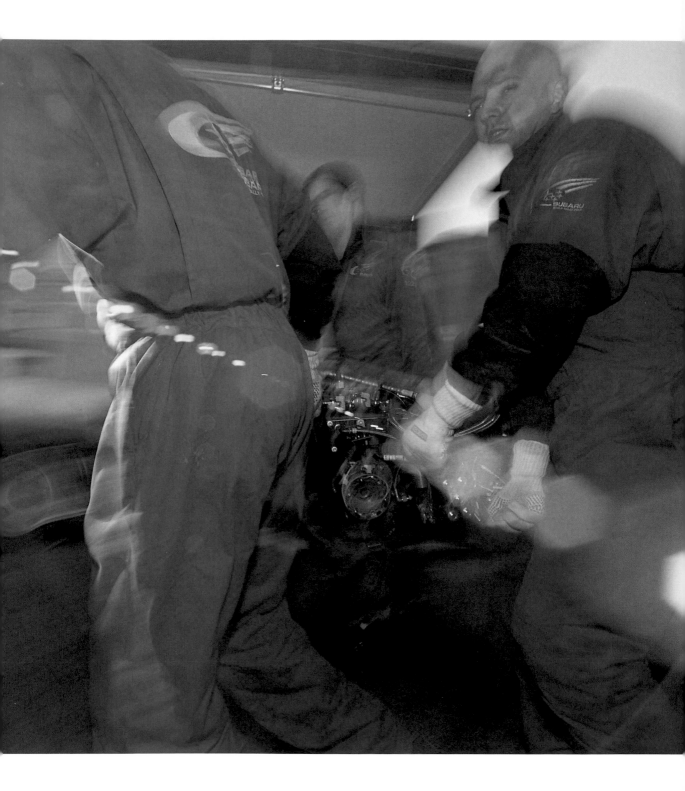

The press always bill the Rally of Great Britain as Burns v McRae. 2001 (right hand page) was no different. Everyone on the Subaru team knew what was at stake

Was it the greatest day of my life? Yes and no. Even now I still have to remind myself that I am World Champion. It still hits me out of the blue. Could you claim that my championship wasn't won by a startling run of victories? Maybe. But it *was* hard, and no one can say otherwise. You won't find Colin McRae, Tommi Makinen, Carlos Sainz or Marcus Grönholm saying I won because I was lucky. They were all in the pressure cooker that was the last three or four months of 2001. And for Great Britain it was winner take all. Even now I occasionally wonder whether it was all worth it.

Afterwards I felt such a massive sense of relief. I know that there is pressure in everyone's life, and nothing I did last year involved anything really important, like someone's health or my family. But it did involve every emotion, stress and confrontational moment that I am ever likely to face.

My Subaru engineer, Simon 'Crikey' Cole. He made sure I had everything I needed at my disposal to win the championship. Everyone worked hard to make sure the car was in great shape for the showdown in Wales.

For example I had to endure digs from Colin McRae, Nicky Grist and the Ford team. I have had to put up with them for years, but particularly since Greece in 2001. It's all part of their game to try to win. But it's not part of *my* game to respond. It is easy to pick up the rock that has just been thrown at you and throw it back and hard not to, but I think I achieve more by sweeping it aside.

Lots of other stuff was going on too, concerning my future. But I created my own pressure: I was up against myself, I was in my own battle, and to come out of it I had to look ahead and plan what I wanted to happen. I didn't want to do any of that but I knew I had to in order to achieve my goal.

Prodrive, who prepare the Subaru rally cars, made it clear that they hadn't given up on winning the Championship. I never gave up either, even after I failed to finish in Kenya. It was really after

Kenya that everyone knuckled down and thought, OK, if it doesn't happen now, it never will.

So we focused totally on it. Prodrive gave me the team's trainer Steve Benton until the end of the year. It sounds like a small thing, maybe, but it was significant because he was employed to look after everyone, not just me. Throughout testing, we all asked ourselves, 'What more can we do?' And Prodrive did a very good job, no question about it. Everything on my car was checked three, even four times. Every engine was built, run, taken apart, built again, then run, taken apart and built again. If you look at the results to the end of the year, my car was 100 per cent reliable. Everything I could possibly have asked for was at my disposal so I *had* to come up trumps.

Friday, 23 November 2001 was the biggest day, because that was when everything happened. There was immense stress. I drove the first stage of the day and had planned exactly what I wanted to do. I knew that in 2000 I'd attacked from the first moment. As soon as I was off the line I was on the limit and within two kilometres the car was damaged. I knew I couldn't afford to do that again. The stages on the Rally of Great Britain are some of the toughest, and the biggest car breakers in the world, and the event is never won by just a few seconds.

Attack! Drive fast, yes, but the 2001 Rally of Great Britain was all about pressure – who could impose it, who could withstand it. This was me on Friday morning just before everything started to happen.

By the end of stage two, St Gwynno, I was comfortable with the car and everything was cool, so my plan was to attack. Losing a few seconds on the first stage wasn't going to destroy my chances of winning the rally or the World Championship, so I had planned to take it . . . not easily, but to drive it like I could drive all day. I don't even know in what position I finished that first stage, probably around sixth.

Tyle was the third stage. I knew it well. The previous year I was pretty quick on it, even with the left rear wheel sticking out at an angle. I knew I could drive it well so I pushed hard. I didn't have any really bad moments, although there were a couple of scares in fifth and sixth gear when I was off the line. Even so I knew the road and was comfortable, happy that I was driving at the top of the envelope. We beat Colin by a tenth of a second on Tyle so my plan then was to stay at that speed.

From what had happened the previous year I knew that my speed was good enough – if not to beat Colin and then pull away, at least to keep up an intense pressure on him. We had already passed Tommi Makinen, whose suspension had broken on the second stage, but I hadn't considered him a threat.

Grounded. It's the end of the road and the championship for Tommi Makinen.
Co-driver Kaj Lindstrom looks on.

Carlos Sainz had problems too. But the time I was making wasn't the point. I just had to put pressure on Colin. Of course, the pressure was on me too, everyone knew that, but I had to make him think I was a threat. And on the next stage Colin crashed.

He was focused on going as fast as he possibly could. His plan is always like that – go flat out from the word go. With Tommi out I was running second on the road and I could see where Colin was driving from the lines he was leaving. I knew a time would come when he would not get round a corner. I could see he was driving across the inside of corners and across the outside on the exits. He was taking huge risks. He was really pushing it, especially considering it was the first day of three to win the World Championship. His plan was to put pressure on me by being thirty seconds in the lead and making me try to catch him.

As I drove past the crash, I can honestly say that I thought, Jesus, is he OK? It was bad, I knew, because we were travelling at real speed. I had slowed down and I was in fifth gear, so I knew that was a sixth-gear corner. My first thought was for him because the crash looked horrendous. Then I thought, 'Let's just get to the end of this stage'. You can't let thoughts of everything that might happen in the next three days take over when you're trying to keep your car on the road.

I was going really fast past where Colin went off: a junction left, then a junction right. I missed my braking point for the junction right, went over the crest sideways, down the escape road backwards and bumped into a pile of logs. It wasn't a big deal, but I had to tell myself, 'Get it out of your mind, get to the end of the stage, drive to the end of the stage.' When I got there I discovered that Colin was out of the rally, as was Tommi, and Carlos was three minutes behind. 'What have I got to do?' I asked myself. Finish in the top four.

The news that those two were out made me far too relaxed as I drove on, but it wasn't dangerous: I knew I could do the job as long as I kept going. I had won the rally three times in a row, I knew the roads. I told myself: 'I've got good information, I've got a good team, I've got good tyres, I've got everything around me to do the job, and I know I can do it. So what can go wrong?'

Loads of things might have gone wrong. It had rained hard all the previous day and it was foggy – but I had won the rally before under these conditions. So, what was different this time? I told myself nothing could go wrong. All I had to do was drive as if I was on auto-pilot. I didn't have to set any fastest times, I didn't have to pull off any ridiculous feats.

At seven o'clock on the morning of day two the car wouldn't start in Parc Ferme in Cardiff, the controlled area where all the drivers leave their cars overnight. I just told

Before and after Colin's massive barrel-rolling 'off' on stage four of the Rally of Great Britain 2001.

World Champions at last. The first of many smiles breaks across our faces.
It was the culmination of so much we had worked for.

myself, 'We've done thirteen rallies up to now, and this is another part of one of those rallies. So the car won't start. Well, what do you do when the car doesn't start? You try again. If it still doesn't work, you get out and change the spark plugs. All the equipment is there to change the spark plugs. Just do it.'

I went through it in a haze. If I'd sat there and started thinking about the consequences of still being parked when all the other cars had gone, I'd have been destroyed. What the people who were there and watched me do it thought, I don't know. I was on the radio, on the telephone, shouting at my co-driver Robert – 'Robert, give me this, give me that.' I felt alone.

Robert relayed to me the information that the engineer in the service area at Swansea was giving him on the telephone. I told myself this was just another test. I had changed spark plugs in the workshop, although I'd never done it on a rally.

Robert got them out of the toolbox – they aren't easy to get at. The car is a flat four, so they were by the chassis rail. You have to take the whole air-intake pipe off – not difficult but fiddly.

The fans were watching us, probably with their hearts in their mouths – they wanted a British guy to win as much as we did. Did anyone say anything? Well, I'm not the best person to approach in that situation. But when we got the car started there was a round of applause and off we went.

We realized we were late and had to really push on to get to the service area and be ready to go. Fortunately we were on the M4, but if we had been delayed, we would have been late.

That evening something else happened. It didn't cost us any time, although it might have done. As we came out of service the car wouldn't start again – the starter motor had failed. The mechanics changed it and we were a bit late. As a precaution they also changed the main switch and the starter button, which meant that half the dashboard was hanging out, right down by my pedals. I had to stop on the road section to refit my footplate and side panel. But again I said to myself, 'OK, that's what I've got to do.' The thing is, what else could I have done? If you look at these things negatively, you mess up. If you look at them positively, you get it right. These were just a couple more tests laid in my path. If I was going to win this Championship, I was going to have to deserve it.

Come Sunday, when I woke up there was heavy rain and fog. But it wasn't a problem: everything went according to plan.

The day started as it always does with cereal, then porridge at the service area. As always I saw Achim, the physio, for 10–15 minutes. Every day of every rally I've ever done over the last three years Achim has come to see me at ridiculous hours to give me treatment before I drive. It wakes me up and loosens me.

The car started first time, nothing wrong this time. Every time you go into Parc Fermé there are big metal barriers and behind them there are fans, 'Autograph, Richard? Good luck.' From the moment you walk in until the moment you close the car door, people are calling 'Richard, Richard!'

It's always cold when you get into the car. There's a heated windscreen and a de-mister with a blower, but it doesn't blow on to your feet, unfortunately. They rely on the turbo to heat your legs (a bit too efficiently in Cyprus!). Right away you start to envisage what will happen when you cross the line on the last stage. But all the time you know you have to get there first.

'Round, brake, turn, accelerate...'
Robert's notes for the last part of the championship around Margam Park, the final 150 metres of the championship.

Between the stages where there is no service opportunity I swap round the car's tyres. I carry a spare, so I put it on the left front. The left front goes into the boot and on the right side I swap front to rear. That day after I'd done it I thought, 'Maybe I shouldn't bother doing this – what if one of the studs breaks?' But as soon as I started to think like that I told myself, 'Do what you would do in every other rally of the World Championship, because this is just another and if something extraordinary like that happens it's not my fault.'

But it was pissing with rain and that can be a real problem in a rally car: when your wet clothes dry out they steam up the windscreen. I found a garage to take shelter. Three or four other cars were there for the same reason. Once, we parked in a disused garage, another time under the M4 by a roundabout. About six cars were there by the time we pulled away, all changing wheels.

Stephane Prevot, Bruno Thiry's co-driver, Marcus Grönholm and Armin Schwarz all said to me, 'One more to go.' They were happy. They were all in their own battles and we were all heading to the last stage.

At the end of the final stage, you come out of the forest and follow the road round the perimeter of Margam Park. The loop is only about a kilometre long, taking you away from the stately home and then back in front of it at the finish.

I knew I'd done it as I came out of that area. I could see the finish line about a hundred metres away, and I just couldn't help thinking how simple it was – just round, brake, turn, accelerate, brake, turn, accelerate, up to fifth gear, a bit across the mud then across the line.

As I went across I said something I have regretted ever since, because it has been on every TV show. I said to Robert, 'You're the best in the world.' And he was, because he had just become World Champion too. But everybody missed the 'YOU'RE'.

Top of the world. The greatest day of my life.
It took a long time to stop me grinning.

I take the car to Marble Arch, London, my first full day as World Rally Champion.
Mine being in pieces, I had to borrow Petter's renumbered car.

Then I couldn't stop grinning. I got out. Loads of people were there – my dad, my girlfriend, Zöe, my great friend David Williams, journalists, big Kev the cameraman. And everyone was saying, 'You can't stop there, you have to move your car forward.' I didn't care. I was on the bonnet, jumping up and down, kissing the car. In theory you aren't supposed to get out of your car in the control area. I might have lost the Championship if we hadn't been able to get the car back to the Parc Ferme in Cardiff.

In Cardiff, we drove on to the winner's ramp outside City Hall, and later the car was taken away by Whiskers, my number-two mechanic. It was stripped down and examined by the scrutineers, to make sure it was legal, and I never saw it again.

Then it was a blur. My sister was there, with my mother, my grandmother, my dad, Zöe. I went through the press conference and, when I was asked, 'How do you feel?' all I wanted to say was 'How the hell do you think I feel? I want to get out of here because this is it, this is the moment I want to keep, and I don't want to tell everyone about it, I want to enjoy it.'

It was weird because it was the culmination of everything I had worked towards. You work to win rallies and the Championship – the job never ends. So I felt relieved that I had managed to win the World Championship, but I also felt, 'Right. I'm going to do it again now.'

All I have done since I was fifteen has been to drive rally cars, that was all I wanted to do, but I didn't plan to become World Champion. I didn't look at Hannu Mikkola and Timo Salonen and think, Wow, I want to be World Champion like them. All I wanted to do was drive rally cars like they drove rally cars. I didn't have my mind on winning rallies and world championships, just on driving rally cars – just the driving, nothing else.

It was funny what crossed my mind when I knew I'd won. I remembered back in 1999 when Bruno Thiry was one of my team-mates. He's a really good tarmac driver. We had to drive a stage that was new to everyone – one where neither the tyres nor the car were working well. I don't know where I was on this particular rally, let's say seventh. But on this one stage, which was 16–18 kilometres, just over ten miles, I took something like ten seconds out of Bruno, and I remember Stephane, his co-driver, coming over after the stage and saying, 'Richard, you will be world champion.' I was surprised – it was so unexpected.

And I remembered the Argentina rally in 1997 when, for the first time in my career, I set fastest stage times. In the middle of the second day I retired and Juha Kankkunen retired in his Ford too. Later on in a bar, Juha came over to see me. He gave me some advice. He said, 'The best thing you can ever do to help yourself is relax, not think, not worry, just relax and drive, and you will achieve what you want to achieve.'

I thought about Colin McRae too. I knew that he would be feeling as low as it was possible to feel. Before the rally he had said that if he didn't win, I was the last person in the world he wanted to win.

Until the point I crossed the line I hadn't realized how much hope I'd been carrying, and with it the anxiety that something might go wrong. In 1999 I had a terrible start to the year then started winning some rallies and got close to a Championship-winning position. Ultimately Tommi Makinen became champion and I was runner-up. But until you reach the point where mathematically you can't win, you don't grasp how much hope you've been carrying inside that you can still pull it off.

So, at the moment of my greatest triumph, I remembered my greatest despair. I believe that was how Colin was feeling, maybe more so. I don't know if Colin has anything personal against me but he certainly wants to beat me more than anyone else. At least, he gives that impression.

Driving down the M4 after the final stage was wonderful. There were people coming past us in their cars, hooting and waving. And then we came into the service area, which was pandemonium. It was a sea of blue, friends, cameramen and journalists everywhere. I didn't feign my elation, but it was already diluting: the really emotional moment had been crossing the line on the final stage. Now that I had finished competing my win was a fact.

My gran made it to the final service area. She didn't say much – perhaps it was a bit overpowering for her – but there were tears. I was sad my granddad wasn't there. As a kid I used to go to my grandparents' place near Oswestry in mid-Wales in the summer holidays. He was a carpenter and he used to let me drive his van around. I was eleven or twelve. Granddad had a great sense of humour, and I was his only grandson. For him to have been there would have made it perfect.

My mum was interviewed: she was a bit taken aback by that. She and the rest of my family weren't used to being in the public eye at such an emotional moment. Mum and Grandma can always bring me down to earth – not necessarily with anything they say, just by being Mum and Grandma. And now their son and grandson was World Champion.

The First Time

I had to pester my mum into letting
me drive. My first chance came at my
sister's Pony Club meetings. I used to
volunteer to reverse all the
horse trailers into place –
my mum's included.
Not many people could
manage it, but I could.
I was eight.

My first rally car, the Talbot Sunbeam

That was the first time I drove – and the horses were in their trailers. It isn't the easiest thing to do but I could do it and I always got the job. My sister used to go to Pony Club Camp in the summer for a week or two, and whenever we took her there or picked her up, I always drove in the fields. When Mum was helping make the breakfast I used to get into the car and find an excuse to move it or go driving around. I only crashed once – into some temporary stables, fortunately quite slowly.

As a kid cars were my fixation. I knew every single one on the road – probably because I read *Autocar* every week. Porsches were my favourites. I used to draw them, pin up posters of them, everything. I was a full-on car nut. My dad taught me to drive properly when I was eleven. I was tall for my age so I could reach all the pedals, and I knew what I was doing. The first car I drove was a Triumph 2000. When I was eight we moved to a house that had a yard and I drove the car around it. The lap was short – about 150 metres – but I did it whenever I could.

Later I joined the Under-17s Car Club. Its slogan was 'For Kids Who Enjoy Motoring and Motor Sport'. I saw a feature on it in the *Mail on Sunday* and we phoned up and said, 'What do we do? Where do we go?' Dad loved it too, because there was a big social element. There were between twenty-five and thirty meetings a year; Dad became an instructor and was chairman of the club for a couple of years.

Club members were graded from 5, raw beginner, up to Grade X, the Black-Belt of under-age driving. Grade X was the peak. I can't tell you which titles I won with the club, but I passed all the general driving-ability tests to go up the grades, and then the skills competition, which was much tighter. I won that every year from the age of twelve.

Saturdays and Sundays were club meeting days. At eight o'clock I got Dad out of bed and then we were off to the club, where I helped set out the parking areas with cones so that people could practise reversing and doing turning circles. The aim was to reach a standard where you could drive by yourself, and four or five of us achieved that. By the time the parents were having coffee and talking, we were in the cars, doing up to 100 m.p.h., pulling handbrake turns, with people in the boot throwing the cones out of the back for the tests. Somehow no one got hurt. Amazing.

Most of the time I drove my dad's company car, which his employers didn't know about. Other people drove their parents' cars. Then Ford loaned us cars for the weekend, and they became the club cars. You could drive them if you got your name down at the beginning of the day. Lotus lent us an Esprit Turbo, which I drove round the Castle Combe circuit. I got that up to 130 m.p.h.

Barry 'Whizzo' Williams was a founding member of the club. He is a rallying and racing legend. He came along to three or four meetings a year, gave people rides in his road car and scared the hell out of them. I remember being driven around Silverstone by Barry Williams when I was fourteen and thinking, How the *hell* did we get round that corner? We were in his road-going, rear-wheel-drive, 16-valve Toyota Corolla, which was the absolute business. It was raining too.

The club hired half the track – the small track was used by the racing school and we used the other side. We'd go down Hanger straight, do Stowe and Club corners, hammer up to Abbey then do a U-turn before coming back down the other side of the road. We were all just kids having a laugh but doing it well. And for kids to able to do this in the first place was amazing.

Aged 19, in the Group N Peugeot 309 – world's youngest ever works driver.

I met the club chairman, Brian Starr, at a reunion in 2001. He owns one of the first Sierra Cosworths, a white one from around 1987. I remember being allowed to drive that when he first got it. Later, when I was twenty-one and had won the National Championship, I went back to the club for a weekend. He was there with his car, so I took him round Castle Combe and terrified him. I still owe him a drive in my current car.

Driving at such a young age meant I had to sacrifice things at school, particularly friendships. Every weekend other kids got together and went to their mates' houses but I didn't want to because I was off driving. You could say it wasn't really a sacrifice because I was doing something exciting that I really wanted to do, but half the class didn't believe I did it and the others were probably jealous or didn't understand my infatuation. They were into other things, music or air-rifles, and I felt a bit excluded.

I hated school – absolutely hated it. I didn't enjoy doing the work, and my mind was always elsewhere. Every day I was thinking of cars. I wasn't a model student, that's for sure, although they made me a prefect at my secondary school – can't think why. I went to Gillotts Comprehensive in Henley and, because it had a swimming-pool and good grounds, it was supposed to be the best. My uniform was white shirt, blue jumper, tie and black trousers. My report always said, 'Could do better, if he committed himself'. I did OK – I got six O levels.

I suppose because I had so much freedom in the other part of my life, I questioned a lot of things I was taught and I got into trouble with the teachers. I was regularly thrown out of the class. I used to stand in the hallway for the whole lesson then have to copy up the work in my own time. You see, in the other side of my life I was so grown up: I was allowed to make my own decisions and take a lot more responsibility for myself than I was at school.

I nearly got into a fight with one teacher because all he did was make us copy from the blackboard something he had just copied from a book. That was an hour and ten minutes of copying. He didn't even know what he was writing. The coolest teacher I had was in college. He took the life-studies class. He never knocked me but always helped everyone with anything they wanted to do.

I'm still friendly with a guy from school, but only one. He is Ashley Agar, and he lived next door to me until I was eight. He used to get picked on at school. He was taller than me and really athletic – good at running and tennis. Some people might have heard of a mountain biker called Robert Warner. He became a downhill mountain bike World Champion. We were in the same year at Gillotts and he used to muck around like crazy.

It doesn't surprise me at all that he has been so successful: every weekend he was on his trials bike. He was doing a similar thing to me.

My parents still live in the house where I grew up – Walnut Tree Farm. It's an old pig farm with outbuildings, which is where my rally cars were built in the early years. There are three and a half acres of garden and fields.

I was never a team-game person. I played one game in the rugby team as a winger, and hated it. I could sprint when I was a kid but that was about all. I just wasn't into teams. And although I was interested in girls I was never interested enough. Cars always came first.

I was fifteen when I got into rallying, so every Saturday morning I was busy trying to earn money to pay for it. I cleaned the pumps at the local Esso station in Caversham, tidied the workshop and cleaned the loos for a tenner. I'd met the guy who owned it, Keith Edwards, at the local car club, the Craven Motor Club. He gave me the job, because I pestered him like I pestered everybody.

At fourteen I went on a great introductory course, driving MG Maestros at the Silverstone racing school. Then as my fifteenth birthday present I went to Jan Churchill's rally school near Newtown in Wales. That was where it really started. After a day there, Jan said, 'You should think seriously of taking up rallying, you'd do well. You have the ambition and the skill to do it.' He said he had sat next to two thousand people at the school and half of them wanted to be rally drivers, but that I was the only one he had told to go on and do it. I asked him what I had to do. He told me to find my local motor club, and that was where I met the people who were to help me further.

I loved my first rallying experience. I had one of the best days ever in my life in that car. I knew then that I wanted to drive a rally car. From that moment on, my time was split between going to school and college, working at the weekends and motor-club meetings. I also turned out at rallies to marshal, helped out as a mechanic and acted as co-driver on road rallies. I even did some stage rallies, because you could do that at fifteen or sixteen. You can see why I was too busy to be interested in school.

My dad bought me my first rally car – a Talbot Sunbeam 1.6 automatic. It cost £400 and it needed converting. Gordon Jarvis, one of the guys at the Craven Motor Club, had found it. I was fifteen. Gordon and the Craven Club had a big impact on my career when they built that Sunbeam car with me. It didn't look great but it was really well done: it had the right roll-cage, the right strengthening in the body shell and the welding was beautifully done. Gordon knew where to get all the bits it needed. He had

The factory 309 GTi on the RAC Rally 1990.

done the Rally of Great Britain in a Sunbeam about five times so he knew the ins and outs of a car like that. He's a great guy – still wears an overall with a shirt and tie. It's difficult to describe or pigeonhole him. He worked at the same garage for twenty years and sold cars for twenty years or more. He just goes about his business, loves rallying and cars. My dad's just helped him build a new garage beside his house.

Mum and Dad were supportive too. They were happy I'd found something to do that I loved and could see I didn't want to do anything else. I was lucky: very few people have jobs they love; most just have to go to work to earn money, not because they'd rather be at work than anywhere else.

When I meet young drivers now and ask what commitments they make to rallying, they don't even scratch the surface of what I used to do: my whole life was rallying. It's not their fault – they have responsibilities, they have to work – but I was fortunate: I lived at home and my only outlay was rallying. All my money, everything, went on that. To me discos and pubs weren't much fun. The most fun I had was with people whose interests were the same as mine.

Ask my mum. She remembers my college routine: up in the morning, off to college; then, three days a week, from college to the local Waitrose supermarket in Henley, stack shelves for four hours, come home, have something to eat, and at ten thirty in the evening go out and work on my rally car until one or two in the morning. The next day I did it all over again. I even worked on other people's cars. There was one over at Bourne End, a Toyota Corolla, that I drove when I was eighteen. I also used to go back up to Jan's at the weekend and help out at the rally school.

Despite all that I still took a BTech in general engineering – but I've never wasted so much time in my life as I did at college.

I didn't rally competitively until May 1988 because I couldn't afford to. The Newtown stages, which was local to Jan Churchill, was the first and I was seventeen. My ambition wasn't to be world champion: the only thing I had in my mind was that one day I was going to do bigger rallies, so I only did rallies that incorporated stages that were used on bigger rallies. The Newtown stages are used on the Severn Valley stages, a national rally, and the Severn Valley stages were used on a larger event still. I always did the rallies that included classic stages. Newtown has also been classic country for the Rally of Great Britain. To take part cost me all of my ten pounds from the weekend cleaning job and the fifteen I earned at the supermarket. In the summer holidays I delivered bread. Again, the money went straight into my bank account to be spent on tyres, petrol and other bits for the car. The entry fee would have been around £250.

Borrowed cars (1) – I wrote this one off in Radnor.
Since then I've made up for it by never being beaten in that forest.

I decided which rallies we would do, and John King, one of the most experienced guys in the Craven Club, co-drove. I think Jan even paid for my Sunbeam to be painted – white with a green stripe on it for the rally school. David Williams, also from the Craven Club, paid for the tyres – I hounded him to help me. Gordon and my dad came along and serviced. The Severn Valley was a one-day rally with 45–50 miles of stages, and I was around number 80, because it was my first time. I finished about fiftieth and fourth in the class, a good result. It was impossible to do any good times overall because I was in a standard 1.6-litre engine with drum brakes on the back, no limited slip differential and a standard steering rack. However, I knew I had all the rally manoeuvres

Borrowed cars (2) – one I kept on the road. Toyota Corolla, Wales 1989.

because I had been doing them for two years and messing around since I was eleven. All the fundamentals – like the handbrake turns – were in place. Jan had taught me and they came easily.

I think the next rally was in Bagshot. It was the local Craven Club rally, an absolute car wrecker. With fifty or more people in it, I finished fifth, which, with the car I had, was unbelievably good. Well out of order.

After the first year with my Sunbeam I realized I couldn't do much more with it unless I spent three or four grand on it. At the end of 1988 I sold it and throughout 1989 I didn't drive a single car that belonged to me. In fact, that Sunbeam was the only rally car that has ever belonged to me. In 1989 I used four cars, one owned by a Craven Club guy, two by Jan, and the fourth belonged to a guy called Mike Chittenden. I beat Mike when I won the Bagshot rally. Three or four weeks later I was servicing at another rally for Beric Ewin. I had turned up in my old clothes ready to service the car, only to find that Mike had been refused entry. He must have recognized me as the kid who had beaten him the weekend before because he came up to me and said we should go to the organizers and get me in his place. The next thing I knew I was competing in his car, doing a rally in a 240-horsepower Ford Escort. I had the best day in that car – an R-registered Mark 2, from 1977. I won my class. Mike got a good deal out of that – but I got a better one, driving.

Now it was time for me to buy a road car. I got a 1-litre Fiat Uno, which cost me £1,600 – a major dent in my finances but I had to have it: I was starting to teach at rally schools, so I needed to be able to get about.

Around this time I was on the phone all the time to another Craven Club member, David Williams. His company name of the time, 'Innervisions', was displayed on the early Ford Escorts I drove. Something triggered him into taking me under his wing. 1989 had been the inaugural year of the Peugeot Challenge, which Paul Frankland won from Kevin Furber. The next year the competition was split into two; national challenge and international. That year there was a special stage on the Rally of Great Britain and these Peugeot championship drivers put on a demonstration. David must have seen it and called me. It was a Sunday afternoon – the first Sunday of the Rally of Great Britain. He said, 'Richard, you have been pestering me and you think you're good at rallying. What would you like me to do to help you make a career of it? What would be the best thing I could do?'

Straight away I said, 'Buy me a Peugeot.' I had known David for three or four years. He had been paying for my tyres and various other things but had never said straight out that he really wanted to help me. He'd always said something like, 'I'll buy you some tyres, but now go away.' Now he was saying, OK, where do we start? When I put the phone down I was shaking. His offer was worth £10,000 because that was what a good car cost.

We spent the next two weeks in November driving around the country looking for a Peugeot 205. Eventually, in February, we found one in Essex. It belonged to a guy called Mike Bell who worked for Ralliart in Maldon.

We stripped it down to nothing and rebuilt it. We painted it – did everything to it. It

Borrowed cars (3) – Ford Escort, Yorkshire 1989.

was beautiful and ready to go. Then we said, 'Let's get it to Jan's rally school. We've got to make sure nothing breaks, and we've got to get to know it.'

I drove it around, taking it easy, learning how it behaved. But David said, 'No, I'll show you how to do it.' He got in and drove it like he drove his Metro 6R4. And he rolled it.

Luckily it wasn't damaged – just some bent panels – so we decided to stay another day: because it had gone over once, we could drive it and not worry about whether we rolled it. We went flat out all day – up and down, up and down. Our target was the 1990 Peugeot Challenge. It consisted of nine events, it was nationally recognized and fifty cars were taking part. And there was prize money.

Mick Shonfield has a garage in Reading called Autocare, and used to work on David's rally cars. That was how we all knew him and why he got involved. When the Peugeot Challenge came along he said he'd work on the car for nothing, as long as we put his name on it.

We decided that I would drive to the rally with the car, do the event, drive back that night, then take all the stuff back to my parents' house. On Sunday I would get up early and drive the car to Mick's workshop. He would open up, I would power-wash the car, check everything was OK, drive it home, take it apart and prepare it for the next rally. As it turned out I even repainted the stone-damaged sills, took off the chipped stickers and put on new ones. It was immaculate.

Mick, Gordon, Dad and I always took it apart, rebuilt it and painted it. Everyone thought we had shedloads of money because David Williams had a 6R4 and he was doing rallies himself. They assumed he was pouring money into me as well. But once he had bought the car, David didn't put any money into it – he just owned it. He lent us his service barge, which was like an old Nissan Patrol, so everyone must have thought *we* had loads of money too. But we didn't.

The Peugeot 205 bought for the 1990 Challenge before David rolled it.

My First Peugeot Years

The Peugeot Challenge:
great memories, great results
and a bloke called Robert Reid.

My car for the 1990 Peugeot Challenge was so immaculate that people decided my team was loaded with money. We weren't. But we were quick. I did everything I could to make sure my car was the best it could be, and the work paid off because I won every rally I did in that Peugeot for two years.

To start with I knew that the lighter the car was the faster it would go, so I made light mudflaps for tarmac rallies but had the proper big ones for gravel – a little thing, but important. Other people didn't have time to do things like that – they had families and other responsibilities – so they just kept the car at the same specification all year.

I was cute with my tyres too. I used to buy them for £60 each and do one, maybe two stages with them on the front then sell them for £40. That way I could afford to buy another set of new tyres for the next rally – and they'd only cost me £20. The day after a rally I would phone up *Motoring News* and sell them on.

We kept an eye on the money. We had a rally account which David Williams held, that paid for all the entry fees, fuel, hotels and what-have-you. But I also won prize money, £800 on a normal rally, £1500 on an international, which helped. Over the year I won eight or nine grand.

It was at the end of 1990 that I met Robert Reid, my co-driver. We were both doing the Audi Sport Rally in Wales. It was the first meeting of the International and National Championships in the Peugeot Challenges and there was a lot of excitement over who would win. About twenty-five guys were doing the International event – supposedly the higher-level people. Robert was co-driving with a guy called Steve Egglestone, a brilliant road-rally driver who had won several and was in the top three of the International Championship. Robert thought he was the business – that no one could go faster.

But I won by about fifty seconds. That must have surprised Robert because after the rally he came to find me. The co-driver I was using, a guy called Jason Murphy, was one of my friends from the Under-17s Car Club, but he didn't have the time to put into it. In fact, I'd had fifteen or sixteen co-drivers by then but they just didn't have the commitment that I had. Robert, however, had that commitment. He came well recommended: he had read maps, done road rallies and pace notes – he had to be the man.

The prize for winning the Peugeot Challenge was an RAC drive in a Group N factory-backed Peugeot 309. I was third in my class and twenty-eighth overall, but I was also just nineteen. I became the youngest ever factory-backed driver. It might only have been a Group N Peugeot 309, but it was a factory car and I can still see my name on its wing.

Immaculate. My entry for the Peugeot Challenge 1990. It was fast, too.

The trouble was that at the end of that first year in 1990 we were naïve. We thought we were bound to get a sponsor and do the Open Championship in a better car. It didn't happen, so in December we decided that we would have to do the Peugeot Challenge again but the bigger part of it.

By now I was becoming known, but I still needed experience so I did other events as well. In February 1991 there was an international rally in Yorkshire, called the Talkland. It was part of the Open Championship, which Colin McRae was then doing in the Group A Subaru Legacy. David Williams had entered his Group N Sierra Cosworth, a 4 x 4. It was snowy and he decided he didn't want to drive, so he handed the entry to me and told me to do it in the Peugeot 205. After the first two or three stages, I was lying fifth or sixth overall, which was amazing. Eventually the gearbox broke but at one stage I had a seven-minute lead in my class and was lying seventh or eight – so good it was stupid.

Then I did the Welsh rally, finishing thirteenth but I won my class again. I did three rallies that year in the Open Championship – the Welsh, the Scottish and the Manx – and won my class in all of them. I won all my championship rallies in the 205 GTi as well. And for those three rallies that year, I was lent a factory-built, 16-valve Group N Peugeot 309 – a brand new, untried car. Because Peugeot's motorsport manager, Des O'Dell, wasn't sure how good I was, they gave me a works co-driver, Chris Wood, to find out. I shook the car down at the Newtown stages and finished third overall.

Driving the factory 309 GTi on the Manx Rally 1991.

1991 Peugeot Challenge Rally in Wales.

Des was keen to help us out – but by now Prodrive, the company who prepare Subaru rally cars, were asking about me. A guy called Martyn Spurrell was working on their Group N Subaru Legacy programme. They had done a couple of rallies with David Gillanders and not been very successful, so they approached David and me and asked if I wanted to drive their car. They said it would cost a couple of thousand pounds, but that the car was capable of winning national rallies.

We did a Scottish National Championship rally, finishing third overall, but at the end of the year, as a prize for winning the Peugeot Championship, I did the RAC in a Group A 16-valve 309, a car that was even more powerful than Group N – 215 horsepower with a six-speed gearbox.

They were good days in 1991, some of the best, although I still had no girlfriend, still wasn't going down to the pub or anything like that. My best friend was a guy called Robert Sutton, an ex-boyfriend of my sister. He was older than me, worked, and had a flat near my parents' house, so I hung out there.

Then came the Shell Scholarship of 1991, a scheme designed to reward the most promising young rally driver. The final that year was a class act: there was me, Dom Buckley, Jonny Milner, Alister McRae, Mark Higgins and Robbie Head – a fair old selection. I thought I had done everything I needed to win and had pinned all my hopes on it. The prize was worth about £100,000 and included the chance to drive a Group N Sierra Cosworth in the British Open Rally Championship, with everything fully paid up.

The Scholarship was a one-day selection test and it examined more than just driving. It included a trip to the Dunlop factory, car-driving on track and gravel conditions, testing co-drivers, everything. On the tour of the factory we were shown how tyres were made, but in the driving I was the fastest person on the gravel and second fastest round the track. (Mark Higgins was the fastest on the track.) The winner would be picked by Shell, some other sponsors and by the people who were judging the driving – about ten in all.

Alister had driven the Open Championship in a Group A Nova. He had done well but some people were still surprised when he won the Scholarship. It's fair to say there was a little controversy at the time, and I felt that, from a purely driving point of view, I should have won. Two people there said I should have won it: Phil Short, who now works with Ford, and Bertie Fisher, a five-times Irish Champion, who was sadly killed early last year in a helicopter crash. I think maybe the judges thought that if Alister didn't win the Scholarship he would be finished, and that if I didn't win I would still be OK because I had David Williams and his money.

RICHARD   BURNS   ROBERT REID

Alister went home, but the rest of us, Jonny Milner, Mark Higgins, all the people who hadn't won, stayed. We all got pissed, told jokes, laughed and had a great night. The year afterwards Shell even went on to give me financial help!

David Williams was angry. He said that next year, it didn't matter what it took, we were going to beat them. We would use his Subaru Legacy.

I don't harbour a grudge against Alister for winning the Scholarship because that was what made me and it made my career. I can look back on it now and think that it was the best thing that could have happened. He won because he is a good driver but at the time it felt as if my whole life had just ended. That Shell Scholarship was the only thing that mattered.

Up to the Scholarship it had been plain sailing, hard work but fun. Now I think, How the hell did I manage to do all that? It was non-stop. But it was the most rewarding time. I have more good memories and more friends from that era than from any other time.

Peugot Challenge prize-giving: Peugeot Motorsport Director Des O'Dell and (left) Robert.

Coming of Age

'Shell Team Subaru' was my team's name for the 1992 attempt on the Mintex National Championship. I drove a Group N Subaru Legacy. Ron built it, David owned it, I drove it. I was twenty-one and still living at home.

I wasn't getting paid to drive the car, but I was making an impression. People in rallying were saying, 'He can drive a big car as well as he can drive a little one.' We became a customer team of Prodrive. David Williams owned the car but Prodrive provided us with the parts and back-up we needed. David had found sponsorship from Elonex, Shell and Dunlop, and other people were helping us too.

The relationship between me and Prodrive developed because I was driving a car in which they were interested and because I was a young driver who was doing quite well. And David was pushing for me.

Ron Hill built the car in his own garage with his next-door neighbour, a plumber called El Tel. Ron now works for McLaren. He was paid to do the car while I was doing a bit of part-time teaching at rally schools to make enough money to live on. It was a time of contrasts. I was competing but still living at home and having the car fixed by Ron and Terry. To me that was quite normal, what I'd always done, just with a bigger car on bigger rallies.

But that year I struggled. I won just one rally – the Severn Valley in Mid-Wales.

My team and I were becoming more professional. We used a rally co-ordinator, who arranged the service schedule and planned where the team of eight of us would stay. We tried different people to see who was best and eventually settled on Phil Mills, who has since gone on to co-drive successfully with Petter Solberg in the World Rally Championship. Rodger Jenkins, who works for Hyundai, was another who helped.

1992 was also the year in which I started to spread my wings and learned more about the World Championship. In Sweden I worked on Colin McRae's gravel notes warning him of any unforeseen dangers. I serviced in Finland and Greece too. We were in one of twelve or thirteen vans filled with more stuff than you can imagine, ready to chase the rally car and take spares to it. I don't think I've ever worked so hard as I did in Finland. It was a four-day rally and I got three or four hours' sleep a night. My job was tough. At every service point during the day I was getting fifty or sixty wheels and tyres off the roof and pressuring them up. It was the year that Colin McRae finished seventh and destroyed his car – once on the shakedown, twice during the event.

But in 1992 I got to drive a Group A world rally car – a proper beast. My chance came after Greece, where I did some testing for the team. It was the first time I had driven one. It wasn't a very important test – something to do with the cooling system, if I remember correctly – and it didn't last all day. We only had one service van and a few mechanics. I did what I was supposed to do and that was it – a few times up and down the road and don't crash.

Celebrating winning the British National Championship.

It was brilliant. I remember the feeling and I remember being in the car, which was awesome. I had been driving a Group N car, but a Group N car probably had 260 horsepower. This had 370 and it was the same class of car that we have now. I was twenty-one.

Back in the British National Championship I had familiar rallying names to compete against with Trevor Smith and Murray Grierson, who now does Colin McRae's gravel notes. They had what you might call 'proper kit' because they were driving 6R4 Metros and Group A cars. I was in my Group N Legacy and, over the year, did better than them, strong the whole way through the year. But I had a lot of hassle.

On the Manx rally I was right on the limit of the car's driving ability. I had lost time earlier but we had been setting second and third fastest times for stages. The road was banked and narrow as I came round a corner – on the limit, fourth gear, the car sliding on its slick tyres. I was really pushing. And fifty feet in front, a Cosworth was rolling gently backwards towards me. I was doing 70 m.p.h. I blinked and hit it. You should have seen the skidmarks! I went straight into the boot. The whole of the front of my car was wrecked.

When I got out I went ballistic. There was a lay-by on the outside of this corner and the Cosworth driver, who had retired, had been trying to reverse down the road to park in it. It was a live stage, which means you don't *ever* reverse. Alister McRae went on to win that rally.

The next event, two weeks later, was the Severn Valley, and we had to put a completely new front on the car. We were under pressure and up against it and had to get a result. We had a minute's lead over Murray when the gearbox broke on the last stage and jammed in second gear. But we won.

Alister was having a good season in the Open Championship. He did one or two events in the National Championship with me, but each time I came up against him I came off second best. We were about to come up against each other on a longer-term basis, although at this point I had no idea of this.

In 1992 Alister won the Group N class of the Open Championship and I took the British National Championship. I think I'm right in saying it was the first time that a Group N car had won it.

At the end of the year, I did the Rally of GB again in the same Peugeot I had used the year before, the Group A 16-valve car. Peugeot lent us the car but I didn't finish, retiring at Kielder, in Northumberland.

Isle of Man 1992, lucky to be in one piece.

Meanwhile, in the background, David Williams was writing out the cheques so that I could drive. After the Rally of GB he persuaded Elonex that if I was given a Group A car, I could win the British Open Championship. They believed him and put up the money for me to drive the Open Championship in 1993. Thankfully, I delivered.

There are various stories about what took place next and I still don't know for sure. David was trying to persuade Prodrive to sign me as a works driver, but for financial reasons it looked as if it wasn't going to happen. Then Prodrive announced that Elonex and Subaru UK were going to support them but that I would be joined in their team by Alister. That was like dangling a carrot in front of a donkey's face. I was so determined to win in 1993.

To be fair, and he would probably admit it now, Alister didn't come into 1993 with the same aggression that I did. He had had a really good year in 1992 and probably felt sure, as everyone else did, that he would beat me.

Getting ready for my first Subaru Impreza test drive, November 1993.

Draw your own conclusions! At the 1992 Kayel Graphics rally in Swansea with Shell Team Subaru, from left to right: David Williams, Ron Hill, Ian Rae, Robert, me, Julian Dalby and Terry Timcke a.k.a. El Tel.

So we were up against each other – and against Malcolm Wilson too. Malcolm now runs Ford's World Rally Championship team and over the course of the year he was faster than me – faster but without the reliability. By the end of September I had won four of the five rallies and had become the British Open rally champion. I was twenty-two and the youngest British rally champion ever, so at the end of the year I felt like the dog's whatsits.

I'm sure that at the beginning of 1993, when Prodrive put Alister and me together in their team, they thought that one or other of us would go on and win the title and they would just have to pick whoever won to be in the team next year. For me it was a crucial year. At the end of it I had beaten him to the full-time works drive and he had to carry on doing the British Championship. It took him another two years to get into a world rally car.

I finished 1993 with the Rally of Great Britain – I came seventh but I was acutely aware that I was nowhere near the pace. It was very snowy and we were on snow tyres for most of the rally – tricky. I was in a year-old car but still not as close as I should have been to Juha Kankkunen, who won it, or Carlos Sainz. I did OK, but I wasn't special.

1993 RAC Rally, Subaru Legacy.

The next day I was off to Thailand to do the last round of the Asia Pacific Championship as a team-mate to Possum Bourne – it was as quick as that. I had been offered the contract with Subaru for 1994 and 1995 and the whirlwind had begun.

In Thailand it was wildly different from anything I had ever done, and I had a lot to learn about the way the rally was run, how rough the roads were – stuff I had never come across before. The culture and food took some getting used to as well. I think I ended up second, but I wasn't competitive at the start of the rally. I was a distant third from Possum, and Mitsubishi's driver, the Australian, Ross Dunkerton. We got up to speed and overtook Dunkerton, but there was loads of dust to contend with.

At the end of 1993 I was happy. I was also aware that things were getting harder: the higher up the ladder you get the further apart the rungs are. But I enjoyed a long break because my first rally of 1994 wasn't until the Safari at the end of March.

Indonesia 1994 - the beginning of a steep learning curve.

Safari 1994 – Robert and I meet the locals and try to ignore the headlines.

Safari 1994 – we finished fifth overall, second in group N.

In 1994 Possum won the Asia Pacific Championship: he started the year faster than I did but I had learned a lot – the Asia Pacific Championship meant I could compete in Indonesia, New Zealand, Malaysia, Australia and, in October, at the Hong Kong–Beijing rally. My car was a Subaru Impreza that the team had used the year before in the 1993 World Championship. I knew I needed to beat the competition in the Asia Pacific because if I couldn't I wouldn't be going any further. At least I had the luxury of a contract worth £25,000 a year!

Things were a little more grown-up in my life too, because I had moved out of my parents' home and I was living with my then girlfriend.

To gain more experience I did the Rally of Portugal in March 1995. I drove a Subaru Impreza and came seventh – not great but not bad. That year Colin McRae won his World Championship. He was one of my team-mates, and Carlos Sainz was the other. The events were split: I drove the gravel rallies, and on the tarmac Piero Liatti was number three.

Trouble wasn't far over the horizon. I had six events over the course of 1995, which wasn't enough to show what I could do. In Portugal I was seventh; I didn't finish the Safari or the New Zealand, although, in New Zealand, a round of the World Championship, I set some good times. I went out because I went through a ford too slowly, damaging the engine fans and the radiator. At the time I was running in the top five drivers at the event, and I began to realize that I wasn't getting the opportunity to deliver.

I wasn't going to get much more either – not in a Subaru, anyway. Between the rallies in New Zealand and Hong Kong, the team wrote to tell me they were not going to renew my contract the following year. They didn't need me, I was surplus to requirements; they had too many drivers, not enough cars.

I hadn't known it was coming, but what can you do? I hadn't been winning anything. I had being doing well in the Asia Pacific Championship but I hadn't won a rally. I was running strongly – at one stage in the Safari I was third and in a Group N car, which no one had done before – but there had been no solid wins. Hence the letter. But it was

Thailand 1995. This is where I found out what real speed was all about.

followed by an invitation from Phil Short at Mitsubishi to go and
see him in his hotel room.

Phil was the team manager. He sat me down and offered me
a full Asia Pacific Championship season and two World
Championship rallies. Suddenly I was a happy bunny again. I had
a way forward, and with this knowledge I drove better and
finished third on the Hong Kong–Beijing rally. People had seen
that I could beat Ari Vatanen, Kenneth Eriksson and Possum
Bourne.

I came close to setting the fastest stage times on the RAC and
finished third behind Colin and Carlos. I was in the same place in
Thailand, behind the winner, Tommi Makinen, and Kenneth
Eriksson, just a second off Kenneth and two off Tommi. It was
one of the best rallies I have done, brilliant competition, mega
brain-out stuff.

It was at this time that I got a phone call from John Spiller, the
team manager at Subaru. He asked me to contact them before I
got offered another drive and signed any other contract. Why? I
wondered. 'Just let us know,' he said. Nevertheless I went ahead
and announced that I would be driving for Mitsubishi in 1996.
But Subaru came back and asked what would happen if they
matched the Mitsubishi offer.

I asked them why they had written two months before saying
that I was surplus to requirements, and I insisted that I had told
Mitsubishi that I was going.

Later that day I got another phone call from John Spiller at
Subaru, offering more money *and* the Safari rally.

I asked him to look at it from my point of view. Why hadn't
the team offered me that in the first place? Why were they trying
to keep me now that I had said I was going somewhere else?

Sideways at the 1995 rally of Great Britain, on my way to 3rd place in a Subaru 1-2-3.

The toil and the spoils. The bike was a Honda VFR 750. You don't need me to tell you what was going on in the gym.

The reason, I believed, was that they didn't want me going to Mitsubishi, because Subaru had already signed Kenneth Eriksson from Mitsubishi. They didn't want to keep me, but neither did they want me to go.

It wasn't over. I was at Heathrow airport, on the way to the Bologna motorshow, when David Richards, the head of Prodrive, telephoned with some tricky questions. 'Where is your loyalty?' he asked. 'We started you off in rallying, we found you, you owe us – how can you do this to us?' It was the full-on guilt-trip.

I said, 'Sorry, David, but I have a plane to catch. 'Bye.'

I landed in Paris for the connection and my phone rang straight away. It was David. He asked me again if I had made up my mind.

I explained that Mitsubishi had offered me the drive three months ago. I had given Andrew Cowan at the team my word. I had accepted their offer. Everyone was happy.

Prodrive had given me the opportunity after winning the British Open Championship to make an impression on the World Championship.

But now I found that I was the number three driver in a three car team and the best and most obvious thing to do was to move on and learn even more in a new environment.

As a driver I needed to develop. Moving to a new set of surroundings is the most effective way of achieving that.

So I went to Mitsubishi.

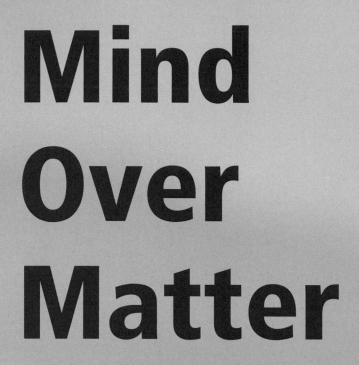

Mind
Over
Matter

I have to have my head right for
rallying. Sometimes it can take a while,
on other occasions it happens straight
away. It all depends on one thing:
I have to feel good in the car.

If I don't I can't do the job properly, so I never leave a shakedown test stage until I have thought, Yeah, that was spot on. That might happen after the first run or the seventh. But I have to be happy. The time I record on shakedown is irrelevant. Even if it's terrible I can walk away, no problem. Of course, everyone is competitive and they want to do a good time, but if I feel that everything worked well, then it's enough.

I can't perform in the car unless I've slept properly. I need eight hours to be fresh all day on each day of the rally. Having said that, though, I've won two rallies where I've been knackered.

In New Zealand in 2001, I had a terrible time sleeping from the moment I got there to the moment I left. I didn't have more than two or three consecutive hours' sleep. That was because of the jet lag. I averaged four or five hours' sleep a night for the whole week, so by the time the rally came round I was exhausted – the second day especially: we had a really long run up north and I was zonked out. But, despite the fatigue, we were fastest on every stage but one. I was just focused, concentrating, and I knew I was going to be the fastest over those stages; I knew I was going to get that lead and I took risks to get it. I know and love the rally and those stages, so I knew what I could do. I wasn't worried about a thing.

If I need a break I can kick my legs out in the back of the motor home – say, in a forty-five-minute service break – and almost fall asleep. I've never actually dropped off – I can't completely switch off, because if I do it takes me half an hour to know where I am again. I was fighting fatigue in the very first rally I ever won – Safari, in 1998. I couldn't sleep at all. That was down to a combination of the work and jet lag.

Unless I'm having desperate problems, I don't take anything to help me sleep. I don't like to because if I did it every time, I'd be addicted to it. I think you should always be able to get to sleep without any problem. All week until the night before a rally I sleep anxiously because of the build-up. It's almost a relief to get

In the zone. I know the car is in good shape so I can raise my game.
Then it's all down to confidence, knowledge and experience.

to the start in the morning and be off.I dream, but not normally during rallies – if I dream during rallies, it's always about something going wrong. I rarely dream about the event itself or what has actually happened. When I dream it is always about oversleeping or the car not starting, something like that. Being late is another: Robert, my co-driver, is there but I'm stuck in a lift, or whatever. I have some fantastic dreams about flying – wicked! In them I'm hanging on to the top of a plane as it comes into land. I have crashed in dreams a hundred times and every time I get out unhurt. Weird but exhilarating. I fly under bridges, or down valleys. I remember these dreams vividly and if I wake up I want to get back into them straight away!

A number of us – including Marcus and Tommi – consult sports psychologists. I started seeing mine in 1996 and he has taught me to forget about the things that go wrong and think about the things that go right. And, he says, when they go right, remember why they went right. He's also encouraged me to think about myself, not about anyone else. I am the only person who has control over my situation, no one else; everything else is irrelevant. The only important things are: preparation, driving and technique. Even if I'm having a terrible drive, there's always something good I can find in it – like in Sweden in 2001 when we went off on the second stage. I had to readjust my thinking, realize I was unlikely to get any points but tell myself I could still achieve something good. And we did. Colin McRae went off in that rally too, but we both went on to set virtually every fastest time from then until the finish. I speak to the sports psychologist during the rally and I see him when I go back to England. He knows what's going on in the sport – he's on the internet, he knows the stage times, he knows the preparation that is needed, so he gives me pointers. He is able to spot areas where I can improve and see opportunities that neither I nor the team have seen. Very often his advice is not what I had expected. Sometimes his tactics appear almost impossible. But they work, which is why I'm not going to go into detail here! He is very good at understanding confidence and has taught me how to put pressure on other drivers rather than myself. I'm keeping examples of how his advice has worked a secret. Suffice to say he sometimes suggests ways of driving I wouldn't normally consider. Everyone in the World Rally Championship can drive very fast. Everyone has roughly similar cars, so 90 per cent of it is down to you knowing you can do the job. François Duval and Sebastian Loeb can both drive cars fast, but they don't have quite the experience. Confidence, knowledge and experience make the difference.

The beginning of 2000 was a really strong period in my career – possibly the best yet. After the first two rallies I won the Safari, then won in both Portugal and Argentina. I knew I wouldn't be beaten.

In Portugal even Marcus Grönholm saw how confident I was. I was leading during the first day but the power steering failed and I had to drop back. I was even faster on day two – only to lose time at the end of the day running in Marcus's dust. But then, before the last leg started, Marcus said, 'Richard is going to win. He's going to overtake me.'

I knew I was doing well. That kind of confidence doesn't come round often and when you've got it you need to *go*. When you know your car is good and that your preparation has been perfect, you raise your level and go for the win. Luckily I know the pace I have to drive at to finish in the top six of a World Rally Championship rally. I can drive at that pace all day. But to go at the pace needed to win requires the next 2–3 per cent. I honestly don't know how you get yourself into that frame of mind.

For me it takes a little time. Occasionally I am fastest on the opening stage of an event, but rarely. I build up to it. Colin McRae is very good at being very, very fast straight away, but a lot of risk is involved in that and he knows it. He will attack and try to get away with things even when his frame of mind isn't perfect.

Of course, I have Robert, who helps make things easier when we are competing. He doesn't let me know about things that I don't need to know about.

Succeeding and trying to win motivate me. I am lucky to have found so early in life what I wanted to do. I also believe that blokes, in whatever situation, are competitive. We have something in us that makes us want to be good at what we do and to show it. However we might try to disguise it, whether we are brash or bashful by nature, we still want to be seen as the best. I'm lucky that I have discovered one thing that I can do well because it allows me to relax in other areas. And I do. I'm a very average skier, a very average athlete, a very average pool player. But I don't really care because I can drive fast. I don't feel competitive in other things. I'm not competitive when I have a game of tennis with Robbie Head, the Channel Four presenter who was part of my gravel team in the Subaru – I don't think, I have to beat him. Tennis is just a good game and a laugh. I'm not a bad loser. I want to know why I lose, but I can also accept that sometimes it doesn't matter how good I am on a particular day, anyone might be better and I won't be able to do anything about it.

There is no one driving in the World Championship who can say they will not be beaten on pure speed. For example, neither Marcus, Tommi, Colin nor I would have said that Carlos Sainz would beat us in Cyprus in 2000. Yet there was nothing any of us could do to touch him that weekend. Colin was in the same specification car as Carlos and had almost two minutes taken off him on the first day. We had no idea why.

Like many people, I have had defining moments in my career. The first was my accident in Finland in 2000. It was the second biggest I have ever had and it was a defining moment in my life as well as my rallying career. First, it was the beginning of the end of my Championship, and second, I had a lot of things going on personally to deal with. It was all too much. The accident wasn't a result of those things but because we were five seconds behind Marcus and I wanted to win the rally. I was pushing hard, went into a corner too quickly and crashed.

It wasn't that I lost concentration but I put the car off big-time. The first thing I did after the rally was go home and sort out the personal business. It wasn't a problem while I was in the car but it was when I was out of it.

The whole build-up to that rally had been pressured. We were leading the Championship and it was Marcus's home event. There was a typical media circus. I asked the team if I could do the normal interviews after shakedown because I wasn't happy with the car and I needed to try out some different things. I just wanted to experiment in my normal way – run the car, stop, change things, run the car again and make more changes if they were needed. I needed to concentrate. But the media whipped it up into a big issue – 'He's leading the Championship, he's wound up, he doesn't care about the media, blah, blah, blah.' Actually all I had said was, 'Let me get on with this and I'll talk to you afterwards.' And on top of that I had things to sort out with my family. Nevertheless, I drove fine. I don't think the accident was due to bad preparation because I still did all that, spot on. But when I was out of the car, I was stressed out.

The crash in Finland had a happy ending. Afterwards I was sitting by the side of the road with my head in my hands, the car a pile of twisted metal and broken glass, when I suddenly realized that a ring I wore on a chain round my neck was missing. The impact of the crash had ripped it off with the chain.

My granddad had given me the ring four weeks before he died. He had never before taken it off, and it was almost worn away after so many years of carpentry. I was heartbroken.

I set out to find it. It was a real needle-in-a-haystack job. But suddenly, as I gazed into the green undergrowth, I saw it. I wear it round my neck all the time. I was meant to find it.

It's not often I do this to my car. This was Finland in 2000.
The car was a write off. I had come off the road at around 100 mph.

Bon appétit! Fruit salad this time. In addition I get through quite a bit of porridge and pasta as well.

Getting my body right

I was introduced to the importance of fitness twelve years ago by Liz Linford who now runs her own clinic. Until I met her I did very little to keep my body in shape. She stressed the importance of diet as well as exercise.

I like my food, everything from a Sunday roast to Japanese cuisine. There's nothing I can't eat, but I try to eat at home as much as I can rather than go out, because I like fresh food, especially meals I make myself. I drink fruit shakes all the time – I make them myself.

Rallying doesn't allow you to eat decent food because you're away so much. Ideally, I would love to have things that are good for me all the time, but as I can't always go into the kitchen and order my favourites, I choose what is best on the menu. I don't go to burger joints, but I do like a good pizza.

Subaru once advised us on what we should eat. Actually it was more a case of what we shouldn't eat and the list included a lot of dairy products, and sugary stuff, like fizzy drinks. I drink tea, coffee, beer, wine and water. I think the biggest change in my diet over the last couple of years has been the amount of water I drink. You can't drink too much. If you don't get through enough, you really feel it. I'm on 10 litres a day at rallies, and as much as I can get my hands on during a normal day. I can't go to sleep without a bottle of water beside the bed.

Best drink of the day. On the really hot events like Greece I can get through 15 litres of water a day.

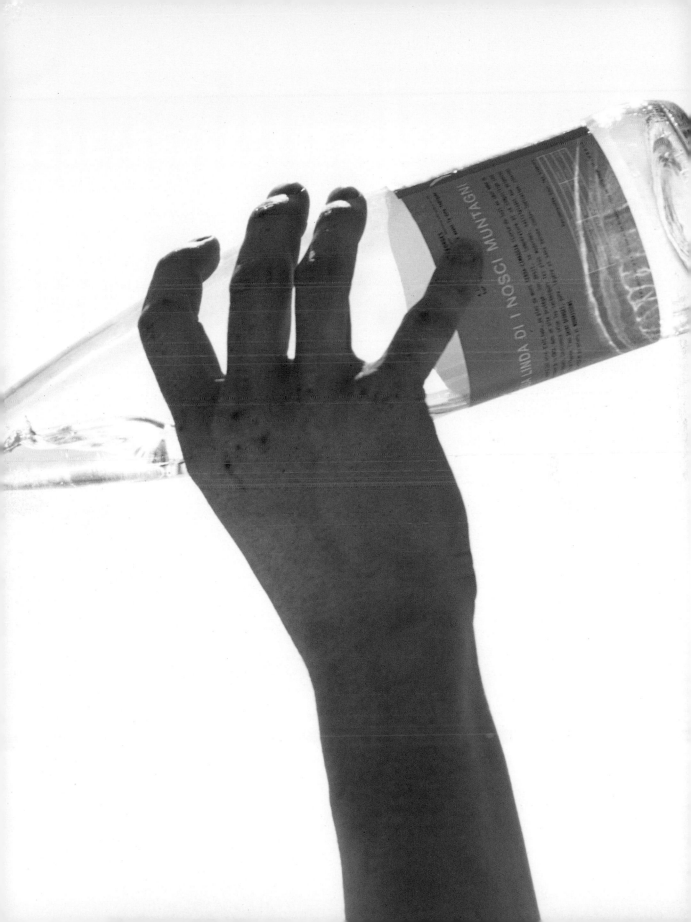

*This is nice. Not so sure about the running. A massage and a variety of training methods
keep my body right for rallying.*

I do a variety of training. We had a very good guy at Prodrive called Steve Benton and we concentrated on aerobic exercise – running, cycling, rowing, swimming and 'core stability'. This isn't really about strength but all the areas you don't normally work on – your back, shoulders and neck. You usually work on your arms and legs, but they're attached to the core of the body, which is where the strength is. You might look at my core exercises and think, Well, that doesn't look much. But you do twenty of them – or even five – and you'll see.

In my house in Andorra I have a big ball, which I lie on – back and front. Rather than doing sit-ups on the floor, I do the same exercise stretched over the ball. It is much more difficult, and helps prevent me being shaken up in the car. I have also done some training with the Formula One driver Pedro de la Rosa. A lot of the work he does is about improving reactions. He lies down in a mock-up of a car with a mock wheel. He receives signals and has to read the signal and react. The problem I have is that I'm not in one place long enough to work that way. Pedro has three months in Spain at the beginning of the season and is as fit as anything.

Getting my life together

I live out of two suitcases that go everywhere with me – one for team kit, one for personal stuff – and I take exercise equipment too.

Every driver and team in the WRC would love an on and off season rather than the on and on and on season we have at the moment. There is no break, and no other sport in the world has that schedule. We hope it will happen one day. It used to be a much longer season in Formula One, before they became sensible and changed it.

However, in rallying the Rally of Great Britain has moved a week earlier, and apparently next season Monte Carlo will be a week later. Because we finish in the last week in November and start again in the second week in January, we only get six weeks away from competition, but in that time we probably have three test sessions to get through in December. December can be the busiest month. All the people who work for Japanese or Korean manufacturers have been to Japan or Korea, there are Christmas parties for the team, awards evenings and all that stuff.

Everyone would like a season to have, say, seven rallies from the middle of February to the beginning of July, then seven more from the middle of August to the middle of November.

There are times now, because of the schedule, when I have had enough of rallying and just want to bolt – normally when I have done four on the trot and haven't spent more than two days at home. If it was adjusted everyone would be fitter, drivers and co-drivers. Now it is so hard to fit everything in – you just can't do it even if you plan everything. And I do.

At home.

The Day
I Thought
I Was Going
to Die

We were doing 100 m.p.h.
There were trees the size of pillars.
We hit the first one at 90 m.p.h.
It took the right-hand corner off the
car – gearbox, wheel, the lot. I've
never been so frightened in my life.

Malaysia 1996 where I came second. But it was turning out to be an expensive season for Mitsubishi.

It was 1996, I was driving for Mitsubishi, and it was a horrible start to the season. The car was not an easy one to drive. The transmission was – and still is – difficult. Just ask Alister McRae or François Delecour. It hadn't the capacity or the strength to lock the diffs when I was braking, which made it inconsistent. Also, when I was in the middle of a corner, with full power on and a front wheel over a ditch, the front would spin. Instead of transferring the power to the other front wheel, the rear wheels would spin, causing the whole car to follow. I spent a lot of time trying to get on top of it.

But by now I was also just getting on with driving. I was happy and comfortable with the Mitsubishi team – the guys were and still are brilliant. I had a lot to look forward to. But early on Mitsubishi weren't too happy with me, because I was costing them a lot of money.

In Malaysia I went off and smacked a tree like you would not believe. I've never seen a car so damaged yet able to carry on. I went sideways into it at about 60 m.p.h. The boot hit it, the rear wheel missed it by half an inch, but it wiped the back off, shortening the car to the length of a BMW compact. We just drove on regardless and – would you believe? – finished second.

From there it picked up. Argentina was one of my elected World Championship events and I finished fourth, collecting my first proper Championship points.

The next rally was New Zealand, which was part of the Asia Pacific Championship. My team-mate, Tommi Makinen, led from the start but damaged his suspension and retired, leaving me up against Kenneth Eriksson and Piero Liatti, who were now driving for Subaru – and I won. It was my first ever rally win in the Asia Pacific Championship. And, importantly, I had beaten the drivers from my old team, both considered very good in New Zealand. It was a turning point.

Now the team were happier with me, even though I'd wrecked two body shells earlier in the season.

The next rally was Australia, a round of the full World Championship. We finished fifth. On the Hong Kong–Beijing that year we came second. But the way in which the result was determined made me mad. I was leading when I spun and nudged a tree. I squashed an inter-cooler pipe, so the engine had no boost. As a result I lost two and a half minutes. But by that time both Subarus were out. Ari Vatanen was my team-mate and took the lead because I had lost those two and a half minutes. And the team said, 'Right, just finish in that order.' I was angry because I had been leading comfortably.

The last rally I did that year was Catalunya. It was here that I had my worst accident. To be fair to myself, I was still learning the car, and running along quite nicely, in about

Malaysia. Because as you can see, I didn't always keep it straight. The team did a great job to patch me up and get me on the podium.

Catalunya '96.

seventh or eighth place. At the beginning of day two the gearbox had seized up, losing me two and a half minutes. But I carried on, got back to tenth, and crashed on the last stage.

We were doing 165 k.p.h. when I hit the brakes, but we hit the first tree at 120 k.p.h. I've never been so frightened in my life. I thought I was going to die – what else *could* you think when you were heading straight into a forest at such a high speed?

I hit the first tree sideways, the car spun, flew up in the air backwards, hit two trees, stopped, and fell to the ground.

The force was immense. Robert broke his helmet on my seat. Can you imagine that? His head hit the side of my seat hard enough to break his helmet. That was a f***ing big accident. But at least we were both OK. The first thing we thought was, Why did it happen? I had been concentrating hard, we were going well. But when we listened to the in-car footage we discovered that Robert had miscalled the corner. We were on a 150-metre-long straight, in sixth gear – top – and he called a 'flat right' corner, that's a gentle right corner that I can take flat out.

It turned out to be a third-gear corner, which I should have taken at 45–50 m.p.h. I was doing 100 m.p.h.

Normally when I go off I swear. This time I just said, 'Jesus.' As I've said before, I honestly thought I was going to die, no question about it. It's quite a feeling. I'd never had it before and I've never had it since.

The car was destroyed, and I had had my biggest crash ever. But I was still young and not even fully into the World Championship.

The atmosphere in a car after an accident like that is one of confusion, then disappointment. Normally I don't fear getting hurt – I don't know why. The first thing you think is, Shit! We're off the road, I'm losing time, how am I going to get back on the road? So you're just pissed off with yourself for making a mistake.

In many ways it is worse for the co-driver, who at that stage thinks what a complete tosser you are. He has been risking his life with you for the last two days, you've both made good pace notes, and then you go and do something like that.

All you can hear is things crunching, glass smashing, and bangs. That's all there is – like a road accident. And, of course, the engine is at full revs because you had your foot hard down trying to pull the car out of the worsening situation. You rarely go off with your foot on the brake because that will just get you into trouble. In a four-wheel-drive car, when you are going off you keep your foot down. The best place you can be is back

Catalunya 1996 – just before the smash…

New Zealand 1997: one of my favourite rallies for obvious reasons.

Right on the pace. Rally of Great Britain 1997 – a momentous event.
For the first time I was on equal footing with my greatest rivals.

in the middle of the road, even if you're out of control. The worst situation you can be in is at a standstill.

Some people automatically put up their hands in a crash. It's a stupid reaction: you could lose your arm if it goes out of the window. We get on the radio: 'We're off, sorry, guys, made a mistake.' The team know it's part of the game, and you know it could happen but you don't think about it.

1996 was a big year for cars. I had destroyed one in Thailand, another in Catalunya and left one in Malaysia needing a whole new rear end.

After the big crash, I didn't have a rally until March the next year, so I went straight into testing the new car for 1997, the car my team-mate Tommi Makinen would drive to his second World Championship title.

I look back on 1997 as a formative year – a nearly year. I was second to Colin on the Safari in March and fourth on every other rally we finished that year. But there were other important milestones. For example, in May I set my first fastest stage times on a normal sprint event in Argentina. I think this was the point in my career at which people around me started to think that I was quite fast. There had been doubts until then.

The Rally of Great Britain was momentous. It was the first time that Colin McRae and I were approaching something like an equal footing because finally I was up to speed and there were times when he was having to catch me. On day one Colin was leading after the special spectator stages. I must have been back in fourth. But the first stage the next morning has gone down in history. I reckon a Subaru with Pirelli tyres is a better car in British conditions, but in the thick fog and darkness I took a minute and a half off Colin McRae on the Radnor stage. I caught and passed Didier Auriol too. For the rest of that day Colin whittled down my lead and ended the day in front of me by a second.

On the first two stages of the last morning of the rally I hit back and got a fifteen-second lead over Colin. But then, twelve miles into a long stage, I got a puncture to my front right tyre. I had to stop and change it, which cost us three minutes. We dropped to sixth, then finished fourth. But I had led Colin, and I had pushed him hard.

A trip to the podium would have to wait. Earlier that year in Africa I had been second to Colin and part of the first ever British one-two. It wouldn't be the last. Winning and reversing that order wasn't far away.

Australia 1997.

The Rivals

In 1998 I finally took the Rally of Great Britain title off Colin McRae. Much earlier that year I had realized I was up to winning. And so did my old boss back at Prodrive.

Three of the greatest of all time: McRae, Sainz and Makinen.

At last, a crack at a full World Rally Championship programme – thank you, Mitsubishi. And now, much more than in 1997, people were expecting this to be the year when things would happen for me.

A full championship meant a first crack at Monte Carlo, where I set about learning how to drive on studded tyres. I finished fifth. That was quickly followed by a first go at Sweden, where, despite setting three fastest stage times, I managed fifteenth place. But I had driven the Safari before and that was next . . .

I didn't let myself down. I took the lead, kept it and won. Another first. I had Ari Vatanen and Juha Kankkunen breathing down my neck, five minutes behind me in their Escorts. The only moment when things looked like they were going to go badly wrong was the first stage of the last day when the car launched into the air and came down with such a bang I was sure everything underneath had cracked.

We were rerunning a stage. I had some rocks in the road to go over. I was in fifth – took the line I thought was OK, but saw too late that everybody else had taken it and eroded the road, leaving the rocks protruding. I hit them full on, really hard. I still had 80 or 90 kilometres to go, another forty minutes driving, and steam was rising from the radiator: it was broken.

Somehow, though, everything kept working for the next twenty or so kilometres so I began to hope it wouldn't fail. I kept going. I got help from our helicopter. The guys in it looked at the front of the car from the air and told me nothing was hanging off or leaking out of the front so I pushed on.

My debut on the rally of Sweden 1998 and my first attempt at its unique blend of high speed and slippery ice – you certainly need studded tyres.

In spite of the impact I held it together to finish the stage the quickest, by five seconds. And I was sure I kept my lead overall. I got to the service, no problem, where the damage was fixed, and doubt pushed to the back of my mind. There was a début win to nail down.

And nail it I did – three months into my first full season. Nine years after I had started rallying I had won a WRC rally. It was a special moment. Top of the podium at last. My team boss, Andrew Cowan, cried. Juha – who had won the event three times – congratulated me as well. That win rated as highly as winning the World Championship. It really did. To see the people's faces. You get a feeling when you're going to win, and I had it quite early. I knew my pace. I still do. My record in Safari is the best – no one has bettered it over the last few years. I finished 1997 in second place, won it in 1998 and 2000. (And in 1999, when I had to retire, I did so from the lead). In 1998 to be honest, not much was going on in my head when I was up on the winner's ramp. The moment of elation had come crossing the finish line. I was then third in the Championship. It wasn't unexpected but it had taken a long time coming.

I left Africa on a high, surrounded in the Championship standings by World Champions past and present. I was third, ahead of my team-mate and defending world champion Tommi Makinen, and behind Carlos Sainz and Juha Kankkunen. But things were moving fast once again. And at the fourth rally of the year – Portugal – Prodrive, who were running my old Subaru team, approached me about going back. I don't know this but I imagine they were aware that Colin wanted to leave them. He had a big offer from Ford to consider for the following season.

Safari,1998: this rally is unique in that I have to listen to two voices – Robert's and warnings from the helicopter.

Must do this more often. Andrew Cowan (left) and Phil Short lift me high after my win.

I was comfortable with my surroundings, though – very happy – and especially with the people. The guys on the ground at Mitsubishi were superb, and still are. They are not a big team by any means but they all know they have to chip in and what everyone is doing. In the heat of the moment you rely on mechanics more than anyone else.

The year before, Andrew Cowan and Phil Short had fought for me to do the number of rallies that I did and without them I would have been down to just four. They were my big allies,

Father's day.

especially Phil: he pulled out a lot of stops and went out on a limb for me. But it seemed to make sense to move because I didn't want to stay where Tommi Makinen was. And I knew where I really wanted to be. Once I had made my decision that was it.

When Prodrive phoned, I had to think what was best for me. If I stuck around I would just be doing things for other people the whole time. So this offer seemed the perfect opening. I didn't see anyone in the team that I couldn't beat or challenge in every event. Initially it was only going to be me and Bruno Thiry. But then, late in October, Juha Kankkunen was confirmed as well.

That was a bit of a shock. It wasn't going to be very good running three cars. But then I thought how good it was to have Juha in the team. Everyone knew his speed. If I could do well against him I could establish myself. After all, he was a four-times World Champion.

David Lapworth made Prodrive's approach. He stuck his head in the car window at a time control in Portugal. 'When you get back to England,' he said, 'give us a ring.' Simple as that.

I can remember our first meeting. I had to do it secretly because it's not the type of thing you can blab about in the initial stages. We met at a restaurant called Dexter's in Deddington, between Oxford and Banbury. I knew what was coming. There was only one thing they would want to talk to me about. I wanted to know what they had to say because my aim was to be in a team where I could be the number-one driver and establish myself.

To call Mitsubishi the Tommi Makinen team would be too simplistic and derogatory, but I was only going to be a number two there because Tommi was on his way to his third World Championship. Of course, Mitsubishi wouldn't have stopped me being World Champion had it been a prospect, but Tommi was on top form and could ride his luck magnificently. Also, he had a lot more experience than I did. It was always going to be difficult for me to reach World Champion status. Experience isn't a thing that levels out, you just keep stacking it up: I was never going to catch Tommi. I felt I needed to come in from somewhere else and attack him.

Mitsubishi never came back to me because they knew they would not be able to match the offer. It wasn't just the financial thing: they knew I was being offered leadership of a team. They were very understanding and gentlemanly about it. And before I left, a Mitsubishi gave me one of my most memorable moments in rallying: a win on the Rally of Great Britain.

We've always been close.

It was Carlos Sainz's misfortune that stole the story that weekend. He just needed to finish fourth or better. I can still see his angry co-driver Luís Moya throwing his helmet through the back window of their Toyota when it expired 300 yards from the end of the stage and the points that would have made them world champions again. Colin and I were rivals, competing for pride that year. Because Carlos didn't finish, Tommi Makinen took the World Championship title – for the third year in a row.

The battle with Colin was close. First he would go fast, then I would. On Myherin I outdid him but he answered back with fastest times on the next three. But you can't win if your car packs up, and that's what happened to Colin. After his exit we

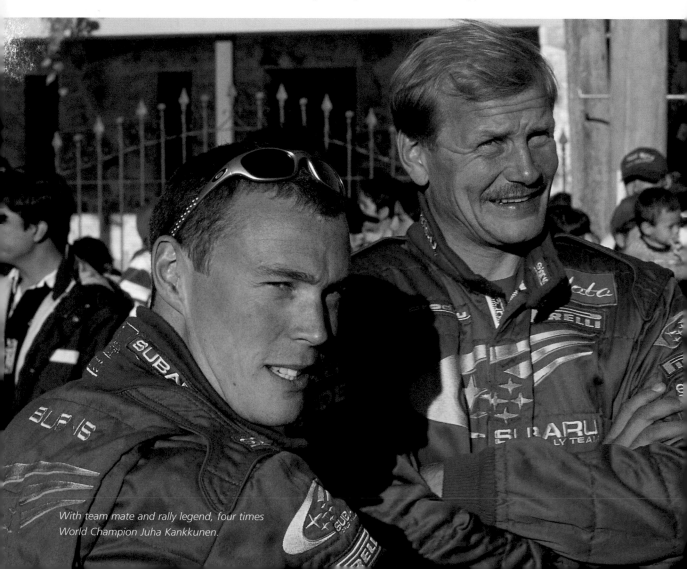

With team mate and rally legend, four times World Champion Juha Kankkunen.

were so far ahead of everyone else that it didn't matter. I won by four minutes.

Carlos, or 'Car-loss' as one paper called him, got all the headlines. The story was about him rather than our win. But the Championship didn't interest me because I wasn't in it.

I still felt I had had a great rally and had rewarded the team. It had been a close fight with Colin, just like the year before, only this time we had come out on top. It was good to take the Rally of Great Britain title from him – he really had been the reigning champion until then. However, he was only one objective. Yes, I wanted to beat Colin at home, there's no question about it, but I wanted to underline the fact that no foreign driver had won the rally for several years and make sure that when we came back the year after, fighting for the Championship, the foreigners would come into the British round wondering how anyone was going to beat the Brits.

It was a patriotic thing. I wanted to stamp my authority on it. I'm able to look back now and say I have won it three years in a row with no one else getting close. To have that confidence is a big psychological advantage.

I had been at rally-winning pace a fortnight earlier in Australia just as much as in Britain but on the second day I ended up rolling the car and losing a minute while in the hunt for the win. I recorded seven fastest stage times to Colin's four and I was in the last stage when I crashed – perhaps in sight of a victory. It wasn't a disaster: I was having a ball.

My performances built up strongly towards the end of that year. Perhaps I was relaxed because I was leaving the Mitsubishi team and didn't feel I needed to prove anything. But I really wanted to do something for them and my result on the Great Britain round helped them win the manufacturers' title that year.

I had no regrets about moving to Subaru for 1999. The people and surroundings were familiar because I was working with mechanics I had worked with before. Juha Kankkunen was my team-mate. Straight away I made him my marker, my target, the man I had to beat more than any other.

It was a difficult period, though. We were all working hard with the car but it needed fine tuning and development. But I never once had to ask myself what I had let myself in for because I knew the results would come. This was the time in my career when I took the biggest steps forward as a driver.

It was up to Juha, Bruno and me to develop the car, but there was a whole heap of things to get used to. At the beginning the car just didn't work, and it wasn't helped by the fact that the Monte Carlo rally that year was difficult. In Sweden the tyres weren't great; when we got to Safari and I was leading, something broke on the suspension; and in Portugal I drove like hell for three days – couldn't drive any faster, destroyed both my team-mates – and only finished fourth.

Jesus Christ, I thought, what have we got to do here? Serious improvement was needed on everything – the suspension, the engine – and I had to get used to a semi-automatic gearbox, which I only got to use after the Portuguese rally. Until then it was an H-pattern gearbox, not even sequential. This meant it was difficult to feel what the steering and dampers were doing because I only had one hand on the steering-wheel for most of the time – it's much easier to feel what's going on when you have both hands on the wheel.

Eventually we got it going. I was trying so hard and driving better than I had ever driven before. Some of those stages were completed at a very high level, and I was driving at 110 per cent. I had to. It was the only way to get a result. But when the car came good, we were ahead of everyone else. And that's what happened in Argentina and in Greece, where I had my first win in the Subaru.

Juha won in Argentina, even though the win should have been mine – my first win in the Subaru: I was in front of him and leading the rally virtually from the start. It was me and him in our own battle – but I was always just in front.

On the last day we were thirty seconds in front of Didier Auriol, who couldn't take time off us. The final stages were really fast. I had a narrow-track car with narrow suspension and he had a wide-track, which was worse on the narrow, twisty stuff but better on the fast parts – on those stages he was able to take one or two seconds off me. But on the penultimate stage I lost ten seconds because the engine cut out, leaving us seven-tenths of a second in front of him with the last stage to come.

Monte Carlo 1999.

The orders from the team to us were 'Drive as you will. You have a thirty-second lead over Didier. Don't lose it! Don't push each other.' That was good because I was in the lead. But Juha was keen because he hadn't won a rally for five years. I went up through the last stage as fast as hell, yet he still took two seconds off me and won by a second and a half. I was mad.

I couldn't do anything, the team didn't want to do anything because it would have looked fixed, and once the rally was over they didn't say anything. Juha did say he would take a 10-second penalty, which would have dropped him to second, but the team said, no, leave it as it is.

He made the offer, but he should not have been in the position where he had to make it. He knew how fast he had been driving, he knew he'd been taking risks, because I was taking risks too. I must admit I couldn't trust him to take it easy. I remember being furious, absolutely furious. But there was nothing I could do. It was horrible.

He became my target. I wanted to beat him to make my mark. Greece was next, and I knew I wasn't going to be beaten there – no way. Even if it meant taking all the risks and chances to do it, I was going to do it. I gave up a 10–15-second lead at the end of the first day by deliberately incurring a 40-second penalty by leaving service late. It was a tactical move and left me to run fourth on the road on the second day. A few people thought it was too much, but I had taken the decision with the team to do it because in the previous year I had led at the end of the first day and had lost shedloads of time. But I knew I could get a significant lead at the end of the next day so the team let me do it. The next morning by the end of the second stage I was already leading and we still had four more stages to do that day. I'm sure the team and Juha knew that I was still annoyed by what had happened. They all knew that I wanted Greece and win it I did – with a margin of over a minute to Carlos Sainz in second. Winning that rally was very sweet.

Celebrating our win in Greece 1999, my first in the Subaru.

The colours of Greece in 1999.

By now the car had been customized for me. I had a choice of narrow-track suspension, which meant that the wheels looked a bit narrow, or a wide-track set-up where the wheels were right out to the edge of the wheel arch. However, a medium set-up was developed for me and I used it all year from Finland onwards. Narrow-track had a great feeling but it was slower. The wide-track car couldn't handle so well and give you the same feel. The medium-track car gave me the stability with the high speeds but had the feeling and driveability of the low speeds.

That year, 1999, I was in with a shout of winning the World Championship right up until the last stage of San Remo. There I retired early because of a gearbox problem, one of many that weekend. But I remember going home thinking that winning the title was still on mathematically. Tommi and Gilles Panizzi were fighting to win the rally and they went into the last stage virtually level. Tommi beat Panizzi by almost 20 seconds. If he had finished second, I would still have had a chance to win the Championship. But he went 23 points ahead of me in the race and, with ten points for a rally win, too far for me to catch him with only two events to go.

I remember getting a text message at home telling me that the final stage was finished and he had won. It hit me hard.

1999 was the first year of a three-year deal with Subaru so I could afford to learn how to drive every rally stage right on the limit. The previous years I had been thinking that I had to get a good result and lots of experience. With a three-year deal I decided I had a bit of time on my side – enough to make me world champion. This time I would start and finish the job. It was also obvious from the beginning of the year that three cars in one team wouldn't work for the whole Championship. One of us was going to go down. Juha and I were hungry, but Bruno didn't have that bit of luck and I think he was always deemed the third driver.

San Remo 1999.

Finland 2000.

To finish the year I won Australia and Great Britain. I knew I was going to win Britain because I had just won Australia. I was also in a period when I had no doubts about anything I was doing. Everything I did with the car was correct; everything I did with the driving was correct.

At the start of 2000 I had to drive the Monte Carlo, Sweden and Safari rallies with the 1999 car, but for Portugal we had the 2000 version and in back-to-back tests on gravel it was nearly a second a kilometre faster. As soon as it was introduced, I was winning again. It was great. I could just feel the improvement, hear it. It was the best Subaru I ever drove.

It had a different exhaust note. The team had moved the exhaust from underneath the car up into the tunnel, so that the bottom of the car was flush. Among other things that meant it was stinking hot in the car – you could have fried an egg on the centre tunnel on the first 2000 car. If you spat on it, your saliva sizzled. We had to put a shield over it.

The main improvement was the lower centre of the car's gravity. It was lighter as well, with improved suspension and geometry.

The win in Portugal meant we said goodbye to the old car with a win and started victoriously with the 2000 version. To do that is rare and it sparked a team celebration. Christian Loriaux – whose baby the new car was – joined John Spiller on vocals as we toasted an amazing rally in a local restaurant. Neither had a microphone but it didn't seem to matter.

Then it all started to go wrong.

In Greece we had damper problems and the engine failed. In Finland I had that huge crash chasing Marcus when I should have just settled for second place. I was conscious of him by then because he was putting in good results all the time. He was second in Argentina, second in Portugal and he had won in Finland, so he was just raking in the points.

Australia 1999: the famous Bunnings water splash.

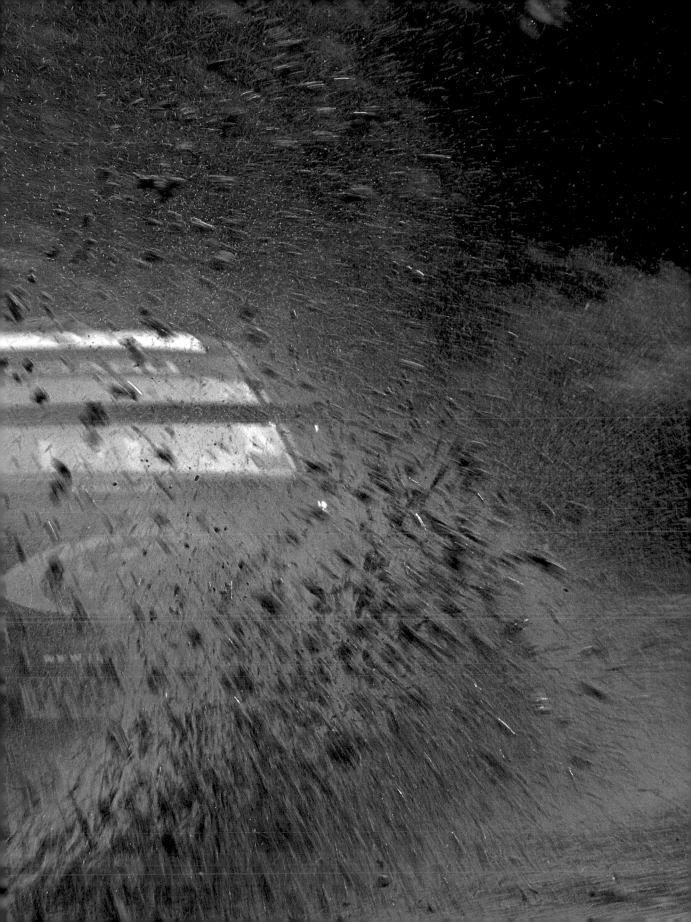

Cyprus 2000, with the new version of the Impreza: it was lighter and had improved suspension.

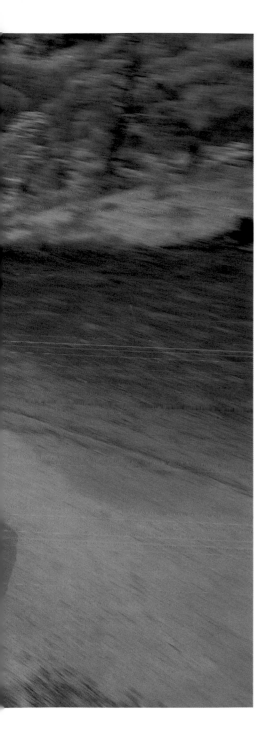

Peugeot had returned to the World Rally Championship for 2000 but their cars had been very fast on the events they selected before coming in to contest the whole season. I really wanted to win in Finland, and Marcus was obviously the person to beat. He had done bits and pieces of WRC rallying before 2000 and had shown flashes of being very good.

Then, after fourth places in both Cyprus and Corsica I failed to finish in San Remo. I was bang on the pace in that rally, the quickest driver on Pirelli tyres by quite a margin, and was lying third. Looking back, I should have said, 'OK, that will do.' But I also knew I had to push to get as many points as possible because the pressure was on. I shouldn't have done that. I made mistakes in that year that I shouldn't have made: they were unforced errors.

We were a second up on Panizzi half-way through the longest stage of the rally, and I braked just a bit too late on a corner. It tightened and I put too much load on the front tyres so I understeered into the outside of the corner where a stone holed the radiator. I got through the stage and still made quite a reasonable time, but all the water was gone and the engine was cooked.

I think I realized my chance in 2000 was gone when I was beaten fair and square in Australia by Marcus.

We were on the pace throughout but Marcus raised his game to keep ahead of us. We had to settle for second.

That set up the situation in Britain: I had to win and hope that Marcus didn't finish. But he did, taking second place, and I had to settle for being runner-up in the Championship for the second year running.

More than anything, the year 2000 was a wasted opportunity when we had the best car. I made mistakes and there were failures too – in Greece and New Zealand where the gearbox popped when we were lying third. I learned a lot – how to be at a level where nothing matters and I know I am going to win, and also that when I am not going to win I should get whatever points I can. I still had to fight as if I wanted to win – I have to have that in my mind.

Simon 'Crikey' Cole, my engineer – a man more English than Terry Thomas – was ready to fight with me over my entire three years at Subaru. He had the same ambitions as I did and stuck by me through thick and thin. I don't know how he coped with me, but for doing it, he's a legend.

I wanted the World Championship just as much in 2001 as I had in either of the previous two years I finished as runner up. I remember thinking I'd been let down by things outside my control in 1999 and 2000; that was why my rivals had a better time of it. But in 2001 I was determined to control my own destiny.

And what happened? On the plane to Argentina, four rallies later, I found myself with three points to my name in the Championship – 21 behind Tommi and 15 down from Carlos. I knew then that the next three events were going to be crucial. Thankfully, everyone in the Subaru team was aware of the situation and we focused on what we had to do.

Do it yourself! Stage 2 of the Rally of Great Britain in 2000. I hit a rock.
Still, I managed to win nonetheless.

Hours of work all ruined after an early exit on stage one in Kenya in 2001.

Things worked well in Argentina. The only reason we didn't win was because I spun on stage three, La Falda, and dropped 22 seconds to Colin. I can't honestly say we would have won, but I think that's what cost us a victory. I was strong from that moment on, winning stage six – the first of seven stage wins. We tried to make sure Colin didn't walk away with the rally. I won stages 13 and 14 by slim margins, and I told people afterwards they could count on me not giving up in the next event. There was no question that we were in contention to win, but we had to settle for second in the end. The six points were really hard work – but as it turned out at the end of the season, vital. Tommi came fourth and dropped points. That helped me.

In Cyprus I was pushing myself harder and harder to win and get 10 points. I arrived there well behind Tommi in the Championship but I knew that Tommi didn't have a great finishing record there. Still, as we started he had an 18 point lead over me.

The first day of the rally was difficult. Ford manoeuvred Colin into position behind me and Marcus. So Marcus was leading and I was second, Colin was fourth at this point, nine seconds slower than me. At the end of the second day I overhauled Marcus and took the lead by quite a margin. The lead was big enough to hang on to – certainly not worth me dropping behind him and driving tactically. But it also meant that whatever I did on the last few stages, Colin was going to hang back and let me start the last day in the lead, which is a disadvantage on gravel.

So I had to do the last day running first on the road, effectively cleaning the gravel away for everyone behind. No surprise, then, that he could drive this rally tactically and even time his win. I still managed to finish second. I didn't think it was the right way to be running a competition but I was now in fourth place behind Tommi, Carlos and Colin. The next two events – Greece and the Safari rally – are ones I would rather forget. Even though I'd got a bit of momentum going, it all came grinding to a halt again. Neither event produced a point for me.

After Kenya things looked seriously bad. We were 25 points behind Tommi, the Championship leader, and 15 adrift of Colin, who like me had failed to score on the Safari. But I never doubted I could win the

Championship. Never. I think our situation refocused people's minds: it certainly refocused mine. I decided to make sure I got the best out of the remainder of the year.

We were far behind with six rallies to go – it was looking pretty grim, and the world title seemed almost unobtainable. But suddenly, from that point on, it was only myself and Marcus who got any reasonable scores. In New Zealand I knew I had to do something drastic to win.

New Zealand is a great place for rallying, with smooth roads and good grip when the gravel is cleared. You can go flat out – the only problem you have is going too quickly. There are no problems with bumps, jumps or the car breaking: generally you can hurl the car at everything and get away with it. Having said that, we still had the problems of dirt and of drivers' positions in the order. At the end of the first day I was in the great position of being able to adjust my placing for the second day.

On the first leg we cruised along to the final stage hardly featuring in the top ten times at all. I fancied running about tenth on the second day because I knew I could make up the time. In the end we finished seventh, over 47 seconds behind the leader, Kenneth Eriksson. But the Peugeot team made a big mistake with their drivers which made things even better for me: they tried to slow all three cars down and ended up making mistakes. Marcus wasn't slowed down enough by the time marker on the stage and he ended up with the second fastest time of the day. This also meant he went off second the next morning. Good news for me – and to make it better François Delecour and one of the Mitsubishis slotted in right in front of us. The gap to Freddy Loix was just over three seconds – the margin to Colin in third was just over 17. The plan was to go like hell all day and to be leading by as much as possible at the end. It worked.

Colin took quite a lot of time off us in the first two stages on Sunday. For the next six we were in the forests and there wasn't even a service break in between the very short stages. There were three stages – each repeated twice, with the two runs through Fyfe at 10.6 kms both the last and the longest. The first time through, Colin took two or three seconds off us on each of the stages, and he got to within 14 seconds behind us going into the last but one – it was the first run through a stage called Campbell. I went

*Greece 2001 and a television camera captures
a shot of me 'sweeping the roads'.*

through it as fast as I could. Colin spun and lost 40 seconds – he stalled it and couldn't get going. So we had a 50 second lead for the last stage of the rally; we cruised through no problem.

I felt vindicated, for the decision to drop so much time, to hang back and then to attack – and once I had it, I'd kept that lead. At the end of the second day there was some talk about whether I should drop time again. It was a joint decision, but I insisted I *could* be as much as a minute and a half behind the leader at the end of the first day and still win the rally. My ideal position would have been tenth car on the road. I wish all the rallies could be like New Zealand. I've always been best at high speed stages.

Even then, as I went into the last stage with that kind of lead, I was still only thinking of the rally – I wasn't thinking any further ahead in the season. To be honest, the goal I'd set myself when it seemed impossible to win the Championship was to finish in front of Marcus Grönholm. New Zealand didn't change this because we were still 15 points behind with some potentially weak, tarmac rallies to come. I knew we'd have a good fight at the Rally of Great Britain and I knew Australia would be very close. There was no guarantee of a good result. It was only in Great Britain that my focus shifted away from Marcus and on to the possibility of winning the world title.

But if I'd thought about the Championship, I would have ended up screwing myself. Marcus was so far behind at that point it seemed a very realistic and simple target, but as it turned out there was quite a fight over the closing rallies. He was getting some really good results at the end of the year. But I can honestly say that right up until the end of the Australian rally I wasn't thinking about the Championship at all.

If we could get you in the back of the car as well as us, this is what it would look like.

Australia 2001.

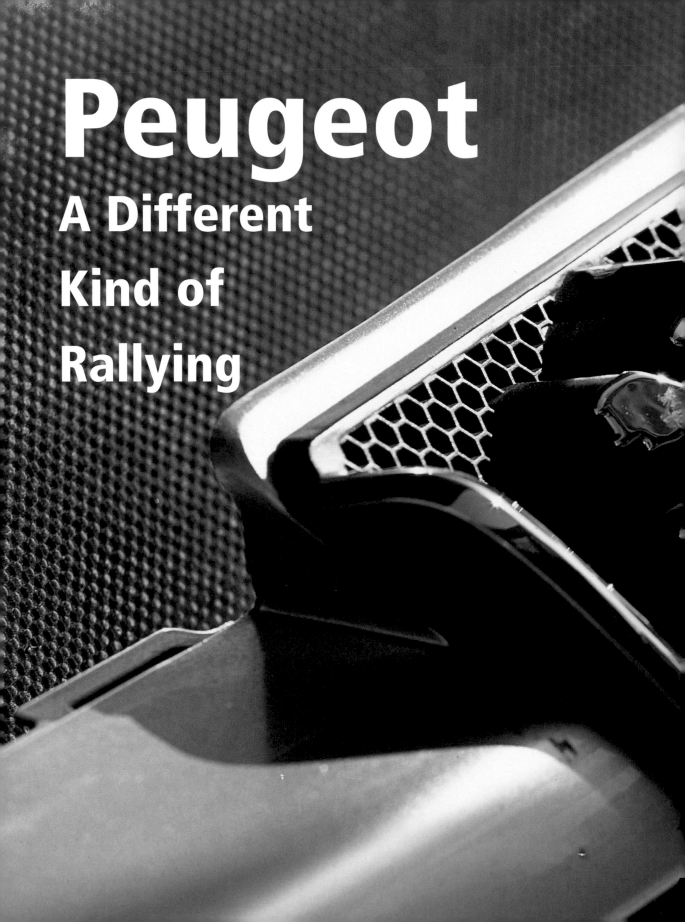

Peugeot

A Different Kind of Rallying

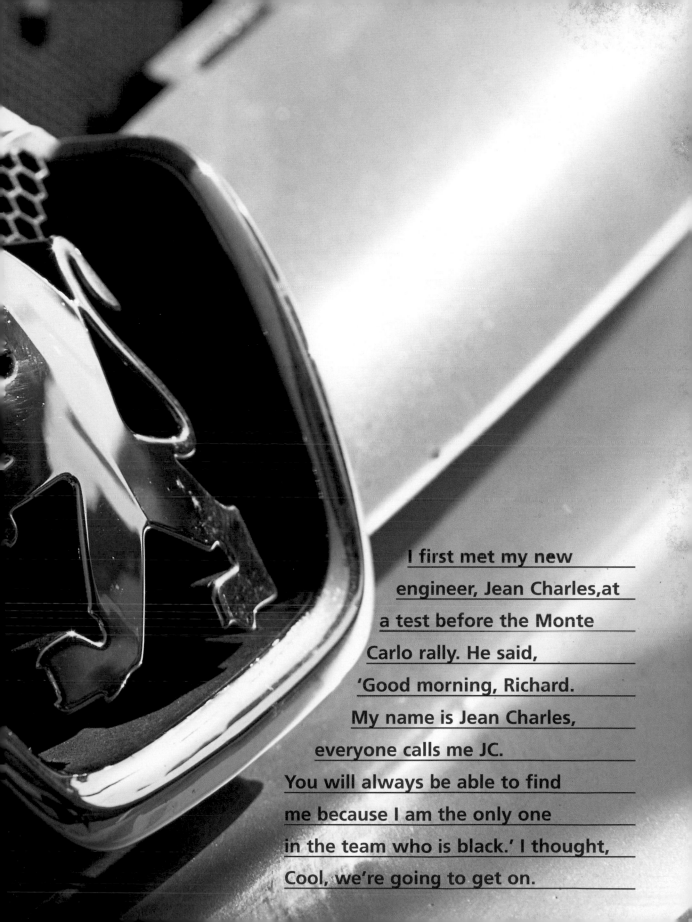

I first met my new engineer, Jean Charles, at a test before the Monte Carlo rally. He said, 'Good morning, Richard. My name is Jean Charles, everyone calls me JC. You will always be able to find me because I am the only one in the team who is black.' I thought, Cool, we're going to get on.

There were moments immediately after I became World Champion when I wondered if I had a future in rallying. I never imagined my life was going to be so publicly debated as it was that December in the Royal Courts of Justice. All I wanted to do was hop into my new car and get it ready for the new season. But 'Subaru Tecnica International and another v. Richard Burns and others' got in the way and that was why I was wondering at the start of this book if all the effort at the end of the 2001 season had been worth it. There I was, World Champion and I felt I couldn't celebrate the Championship at all.

Having Zöe at my side was a huge help. I needed people around me I could trust and talk to and she was best at both. I met Zöe for the first time the summer of 2001 and we've been pretty much inseparable ever since. When all my dirty washing came out in the court case, she was there to reassure me that I was doing the right thing.

All smiles: Jean Pierre Nicolas (left) and Corrado Provera at the beginning of the 2002 season.

JPN looks on with Zöe as Simon Davison from my gravel crew tells me where I could save a second or two in Corsica.

Peugeot first approached me at the Portugal rally in 2000. I met Corrado and Jean-Pierre Nicolas for coffee. They wanted me to drive for them in 2001 but they couldn't have me and, to be honest, I didn't really want to go in 2001. Anyway, they phoned my management company and said that they wanted a chat. They asked when I was available, told me what they would pay me to drive for them. I was exactly the type of person they wanted in their team, they said. It was that clear cut. And to mark their approach, I proceeded to blow Marcus into the weeds on the rally – well, maybe not into the weeds, but I won.

I wasn't expecting any offers at that time, because I was only into the second year of my three-year contract with Subaru and felt I had a job to do where I was. My reply was thanks, fantastic offer, but first of all I can't and second I want to win the World Championship with Subaru.

Tell me another one. Corrado shares a funny story while waiting
for the next stage time to come into the Peugeot team HQ.

You always have to remain a little cynical about these things, though. I didn't think for one minute that I was the only person they were approaching. I don't know that, and I don't want to insult them by thinking that, but in the back of my mind I thought they were probably talking to Tommi and Colin or Carlos.

Also, it is harder to defend a World Championship than to win it, especially if you come into it thinking that the defence is going to be no problem. The hardest thing people struggle with is accepting that you are in exactly the same place that you were in the year before. You might have another year's experience but you are back to zero whether you race with a number 1 or a number 12. Being World Champion boosts your

In-flight entertainment. You can't beat rallying for this. I prepare for landing on a fast section in Sweden.

Corrado Provera: *he and his cigar are seldom parted.*

confidence but it doesn't make a difference to your driving.

I have become a target, but when I do something good, suddenly it's because I'm World Champion.

The fact is I'm in a new situation now, with new things and new people. World Champion or not, I have to concentrate on doing my bit of the job as well as I can. There's a lot for me to absorb – tyre performance, the car, the people, and what is going to help me get the best out of the team. I can't do all of that straight away: it isn't possible.

I might not be in a position to win rallies after just a handful of events but I know the car's going to be fast so I'm going to prepare myself for any opportunity that comes along. So, for 2002, I haven't been going into each rally thinking I'm going to be third, second or even win. Instead I tell myself the car is set up nicely, I can push it, and if I can improve it something might happen. It sounds a bit boring breaking it down like that because all I really want to do is get the most out of the car. I have had a great start to 2002, but the start to 1998 was better: I was second in the Championship after the Safari rally that year.

But our sporting director, Corrado Provera, keeps our feet on the ground. He pointed out after the Spanish rally that Peugeot finished first and second and got full manufacturers' championship points in Corsica and Spain in 2001. They even won in Sweden, although Harri Rovanpera wasn't nominated for points. So, all we were doing early in 2002 was matching what they had done last year, not exceeding it. Corrado is in his element when Peugeot are winning. He chomps on his cigars and loves the drama of it all, but he also knows the facts and how to keep things on an even keel. There aren't too many above him in Peugeot, just Frédéric St Géours, the director general, and he oversees all of the company. However, no one plays with the media like Corrado. He gets their attention and helps to create a good atmosphere.

*Let the show begin. The seven manufacturers in the championship
line up in Monte Carlo before the start of the 2002 season.*

Leaving Monte Carlo – starting the first kilometre after the ceremonial start.
In all I will drive over 60,000 kilometres a season, not including testing.

In many ways my first two weeks with the new team were a nightmare. Because of the delay in getting into the car for the first time I had a horrible schedule in January 2002. It read something like: Monday, fly to Sweden from Barcelona (it took all day); Tuesday and Wednesday, test the car; Thursday morning, fly to London, spend all day there, fly to Paris in the evening; interviews the next morning, followed by the official Peugeot press launch; Saturday and Sunday morning off; fly to the South of France Sunday afternoon. Monday, Tuesday and Wednesday – recce, very ridiculous – 14-hour days with 800 kilometres (500 miles) to do each day.

We were scheduled to make two passes through the Monte Carlo rally route but somebody, somewhere decided it should be three. So, we had four stages to do three times in 14 hours, and again the next day. And this was my first time in the Peugeot. It was hard, a baptism of fire, and on the day I left Barcelona I got gastroenteritis, which I couldn't shake off until the end of the recce. I had a severe headache and diarrhoea. I spent the days throwing up and the nights unable to sleep.

I was so happy when the Monte Carlo rally finished. Eighth place wasn't too bad, really, and I was happy to get round, but it wasn't the way to start a championship. The way to get used to a new car is to do what Tommi did: get into it straight after the end of the Rally of Great Britain the previous year. But there was a two-week delay before I could get into the car because of the problem with my contracts.

The rally routine with Peugeot starts at a Sunday lunchtime when I'm leaving home in Andorra for Barcelona airport. Our recce car is waiting at the airport at the other end, whether it be Nice or Jyvaskyla. I take it to the hotel, where I eat, sleep and prepare for Monday morning . . .

Is it that time already? A rally week always includes very early alarm calls.

Monday starts with a six thirty alarm call, after which we might drive anything from 500 – 600 kilometres (300–350 miles) – that includes every bit of road we're going to drive over competitively in the coming week. We do every stage twice. As we go, I dictate to Robert the pace notes from what I see on the roads. On the second run-through, he reads them back to me and we fine-tune them. That takes a couple of days, maybe three.

On Wednesday evening we may have a press function, and then it's dinner. Quite a few people stay in the same hotel so I might have dinner with Robert, Markko Martin or his co-driver, Michael Park (a.k.a. 'Beef'). I used to compete against Beef in the Peugeot Challenge back in the early 1990s. On other rallies it might be Martin Rowe or Mark Higgins. Sometimes it's Colin, if we're in the same hotel.

Rally hotels are never quiet: they are busy with team members and officials. Some are dreadful places, particularly the ones near the recce stages. The places near the stages in Monte Carlo are pretty gruesome. My favourites are the family-run businesses. There are very good ones in Corsica and Argentina.

On Thursday mornings we are up and in the rally cars at 7.45 a.m., ready for the shakedown stage. Here we test the car on a 3–5-kilometre stage provided by the organizers. We will have tested the car already and decided on our set-up, but there may be a last-minute adjustment to make. A post-build test in Paris will normally have taken care of this and the car will have already been around the test track in Paris and completely checked out. Nothing should go wrong at shakedown.

Rally week means wearing team clothing. The Peugeot uniform is much better than any other team's. It feels good and looks great on us all. The designers did well to make it fit me. With my long arms, thin body and big shoulders, I'm a strange shape. It was all a bit different in the old days with Mitsubishi: then I went with Linda Cowan to the Rugby town centre gentlemen's outfitters to buy grey flannels and a blazer for the prize givings.

*Move it, move it! Dramatic pictures that capture the team working on my car during a service
break. Mostly they have 20 minutes to put things right and often they are required to replace large
sections of the suspension and transmission.*

Rally drivers probably don't look after their mechanics as well as they should – I'm still learning the first names of the guys in my team as Peugeot rotate their mechanics among the drivers. (At Subaru I had the same number-one mechanic for three years, which was great, because I got to know him so well.) They prefer to operate in that way because it avoids competition building in the team. Not many mechanics do all 14 events, perhaps six or eight, so you can't have them for the whole season. Peugeot is the only team in the World Championship in which all its mechanics fly business class. It's a fair shout: they work longer hours than us, that's for sure.

I first met my engineer Jean Charles, or JC, at a test before Monte Carlo in December 2001. He said to me, 'Good morning, Richard. My name is Jean Charles. Everybody calls me JC. You will always be able to find me because I am the only one in the team who is black.' I thought, Cool, we're going to get on.

My relationship with my engineer is crucial. JC used to compete at national level as a long jumper and was at the 1991 Student Games in Sheffield, so he knows about competition. He wants to win. He is very motivated, very clever, and he speaks very good English. So, he seems to be all the things that an engineer should be. You need a good engineer. Things have to move fast when there's work to be done on the car during service.

When I come back off a stage I get straight into the motor home. That's when I eat and talk to my gravel crew and the engineer. I have 20 minutes to tell him what's going on in the car and where I think improvements can be made.

The motor home at Peugeot is different from those of other teams. Drivers are encouraged to stay outside more so that divisions aren't created between the team and the driver.

Your team-mate is the guy you most want to beat. Gilles Panizzi is very reasonable, even though he knows I'm out to beat him. I've even asked him what tyres he was going to choose for an opening stage of the day. He doesn't mind me asking, he's

*Team mates and rivals: I line up with 2000 World Champion Marcus Grönholm
and (centre) French tarmac ace, Gilles Panizzi.*

totally cool – but he doesn't have to give me the information.

Marcus is everyone's biggest rival. I asked him once if he had three kids – that's how close we are, or not. He's not a big talker, even though his and his co-driver Timo's English is good. But team-mate relationships are always difficult: you don't trust anything the other says, not because they are lying but because they don't want to give anything away.

We might talk a bit about our personal lives with each other because, after all, there aren't many people who understand exactly what we do and what we go through as rally drivers so at least we can relate to each other.

I used to worry about other drivers and what they were doing. I don't think about that any more. If you do things to the best of your ability and have confidence in yourself you will win. If I worry about other people I might pick up one or two things but the fact is that I am in the position I am in because I have worked at it – so I can trust that some of the decisions I make on my own are going to be the right ones.

To help us all, Peugeot have six or eight weather crews out on the stages, waiting and reporting. Sometimes they camp out the night before we drive through. At some events there is even a meteorologist in the team: he comes with satellite maps and weather details and can even predict how many millimetres of rain will fall.

It was obvious they knew what they were doing when they came into rallying in 2000 with such a big bang.

Working for a French team does leave you feeling a bit separated from everyone else. Unlike Ford, Subaru and Mitsubishi, Peugeot are not a British-based team so there was almost a feeling of 'us against them'. Citroën are now viewed a bit like Peugeot were, as a separate entity to the rest of the World Championship.

I am not allowed to describe what happened at the end of 2001 but I will say this: it didn't end the way anyone wanted it to. The reasons I moved weren't clear in the beginning. People

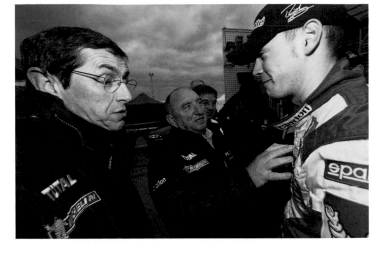

Teamwork The Peugeot team advise me on set-up and tactics. I get the thoughts of (top) JPN and team manager, Francois Chatriot, (middle) my engineer, JC. And then (bottom) Robert and I compare notes with Gilles.

Everyone has their say at a team briefing.

must have wondered why I left a team with which I had just won the World Championship. But I had achieved with Subaru what I had set out to achieve with them. Second, I had driven for them for three years, moved to Mitsubishi for three more, then returned to Subaru for another three. So I was in a comfort zone – which was great – but I thought I had to develop personally by switching. The world is a bigger place than rallying and it isn't always that great to be in that nice little comfort zone. I needed a challenge. I wanted to know what was on the other side of the fence. It's not like this team was a girlfriend I was dumping. It was because I saw a big future with Peugeot.

The early signs have been very good. I didn't get out of the car after the first drive and think, What *have* I done?

Years ago, at the end of my first period with Subaru, I was offered a test drive with Ford. I turned them down. They were stunned, couldn't understand why I did not want to go and try the car. But the test was on an airfield. 'What,' I said, 'am I going to learn from driving a car around an airfield?' What was I going to gain from it? Apparently I'm the only person ever to turn down a test drive with Ford.

So, for the same reason, a Peugeot will go fast regardless of what I do.

Whatever happens, I know I am lucky to have the chance to drive fast in the kind of cars we use. In Kenya in 2001 I went out to dinner with Colin McRae. I remember saying, 'Look at us. We're the luckiest buggers in the world, aren't we?' It was a big but realistic admission. Without rallying, we would be nothing.

But even as World Champion, I still keep up a few habits I've had since the early days. One is to make a call to my parents from the car on the road section after the last stage of a rally. I used to do it when I got back to the hotel. In all that time, after all that has happened, they haven't changed. They're just proud of me.

My mum is one of those mums who can't stop herself asking me if I've got a clean vest on. Or when I talk to her about what I've got planned, she'll say, 'Oh, are you sure you want to do that?'

Mums. Don't you just love them?

Catalunya 2002.

The Future

My immediate future lies with Peugeot,
but beyond that, who knows?
Right now I'm making the best of
what I have.

I signed for Peugeot because I wanted to do something different. They've got a great car and driving for a foreign team is something no British driver has done before. I also recognize that 12 years ago it was Peugeot that springboarded me into rallying in the first place. I'm not doing this as a repayment or a favour, but I am a tiny bit sentimental. It would have made the late Des O'Dell's day to see a British World Champion driving for Peugeot.

Thinking too far ahead is a distraction at the moment because I want to be focused on what I'm doing. Things that have happened in my life in the last year have improved it significantly. What a friend once said about becoming thirty is true for me: I might not know what I want but I now know what I don't want. I'm making a big effort to cut out things I don't want that are a distraction.

I haven't any idea what I will do when I stop driving. I've got my eyes on a fantastic pub near to where I used to live. I could always pull pints.

It would be nice to end my career with a complete collection of all the different cars in which I have won. Over the years I've collected a Mitsubishi Evolution 5, the road version of the last Mitsubishi I drove, and a Subaru RB5 (a version of the Impreza named after me – hence the RB). I also have three or four of my old rally cars.

Drivers become attached to the cars in which they win: they have been through a lot together. Mine are part of the reason for my success. One day I would like to own the 205 in which I won the Peugeot Challenge. Juha Kankkunen has brought together many of his past rally cars to form a collection, but I might have to win another couple of titles before I can do that!

Away from it all. Zöe and I chill out together.

What I drive away from rallies is important. In Andorra I keep a Mercedes ML55 – 5.5-litre, 350 brake horsepower, and very impressive. It goes like hell and sounds great and that's why I want it, not because it allows me to swagger up outside a hotel and think, Park that! I've customized it with a set of furry black dice, like you might have seen in a seventies Capri or Escort. I've hung them over the rear-view mirror! I know the image a Merc can create, so if mine does, I've got the dice to be ironic about it. They're not what you would expect to find in a car like that and I love that kind of thing.

The first Porsche GT3 I bought got the same treatment: I played a Britney Spears CD in it very loud. It brought me back down to earth. When I was growing up, I loved Porsches.

I don't own a Ferrari. They sound gorgeous, but I'm not a Ferrari person. There's an even worse image that goes with them. I have a 1969 Camaro 396SS. They're so rare, they don't even have an image!

In Oxfordshire I used to keep a figure of Mr Potato Head from *Toy Story* on a shelf in the lounge. Let's face it, he's the last thing you'd expect in a 500-year-old Cotswold pile.

I have toyed with the idea of doing something completely different in the future. I'm serious about trying to use my driving skills to do something for road safety. The title 'World Rally Champion' carries some clout. The way most people drive on the motorway is terrible. Why can people in England take a test and then go straight out and drive on the motorway?

In travelling the world with the WRC I have realized how beautiful it can be. I like England and my long-term future lies there, but even in Andorra or Barcelona I have to remind myself sometimes what time of year it is because the weather around

Eclipsed. I first met Zöe in 2001. Since then we've been pretty much inseparable.

the Mediterranean is so good in winter. Occasionally I picture the house I will live in when my career is over. It will be surrounded by English countryside and, no doubt, my love of the ironic will be seen there too.

Andorra is my home for now, and I love it. It's very private, I enjoy the Spanish way of life and I appreciate the attitude of the Spanish people. I like Monaco, but only for a two- or three-day stay. It's too ostentatious for me to contemplate living there permanently. In Andorra I can train well because the weather is good. I love Barcelona too, so sometimes I stay there for a couple of days just for the hell of it.

I have got a lot and I appreciate it – the woman I love, a great home and some awesome cars. No, it's not the lad-abroad hard-partying lifestyle that many would choose, but I'm happy with it. There are many things I should have done earlier. I wish I'd lived abroad when I was younger. I've learned so much about myself from not being in England. It's been very educational getting to know me!

I can't see myself doing a Juha Kankkunen or Stig Blomqvist, still driving in my forties and fifties, although I like the way Juha accepts occasional offers to drive reasonably competitive cars in his favourite rallies! I could be tempted to do that.

I admire Carlos. He's one of the fittest, most determined and most professional drivers, and he's very intelligent. I also think he could do a fantastic job for rallying if he wasn't driving.

I don't fear injury ending my rallying career, even when I think of what happened to me in Catalunya and Finland. I know it sounds boring but I don't take myself over the limit where I know I'm in control.

*Back where it all started. I join Justin Dale (right) for the start of
the 2002 British Championship.*

My partnership with Robert Reid could last all the way through. I have no reason to change co-drivers. He knows everything, so much so that if we go down a road section and someone turns right but Robert tells me to go straight on, I go straight on. He is so good I don't question him, even if it looks like I should. He is, without doubt, the best person in the world on pace notes, their delivery and clarity. He never misses a beat, rarely has to repeat anything and understands what the car is doing all the time. Brilliant. I have ultimate trust in him just as I do in Simon and Steve, my gravel crew. For the last four years I've also had a PA, Clare Caudwell, who's taken a tremendous amount of work away from me. These people do everything they can for me, short of being my family. They have my interests at heart.

And I am the marrying kind – which will please my grandmother, because she is always badgering me about when I'm going to put a ring on Zöe's finger. I'm a fan of the whole white-wedding thing and having a family too. But I think I'll be terrified on the day. I was a guest at Michael Park's wedding in 1993. When he knelt down at the altar, he had HELP written on the soles of his shoes!

My life in the World Rally Championship is a far cry from the way it was as a 15 year-old. As a teenager I never looked that far into the future and pictured myself doing what I'm doing now. All I wanted to do then was to drive a rally car. Now I'm doing it with the best team in the world. And this is how Robert and I start each stage that we are competing on.

Robert checks the car's tyre pressures. They can rise on a stage and then fall on the road sections. Often I need to warm them up a bit and improve their grip. So, I weave my way down to the stage start - sharp acceleration, hard on to the brakes, swerving

to the left and right. At the start I turn off the car and wait. Then I go into my routine - earplugs in, balaclava on, do up the safety belts.

Helmet on - plug in the intercom - there are two plugs: one that goes from the earplugs to the helmet, one from the helmet to the intercom. Suck on my drinks tube - the first mouthful is warm, the top of the tube is exposed to the heat.

Now I start the car - ignition switch on, fuel pump on, foot on the clutch, press the start button. Check my notes for what's coming up. From here on we have no contact with the team. Robert and I are on our own.

Time to line up for the stage, being careful not to break the infrared beam that cuts across the road (it stops anyone from jumping their official start time).

Wait...think...breathe...concentrate...

15 seconds to go: I put the car in gear.

10 seconds to go: I turn on the antilag switch -
this will give me an instant response from the
engine...select first gear.

5 seconds to go. Press the blue launch control button
on the right hand side of the steering wheel,
floor the throttle and get the engine to full boost.

ZERO - up comes the clutch. I tilt my head forward,
ready to absorb the acceleration. Through the gears,
up to speed...relax and drive...nought to sixty
in four seconds...

Richard Burns
Vital Statistics

1989

Toyota Corolla GT	Panaround	30th
Ford Escort	Bagshot	1st
Ford Escort	Mid-Wales	12th
Ford Escort	Millbrook	11th
Ford Escort	Severn Valley	R
Toyota Corolla GT	Kayel Graphics	R
Toyota Corolla GT	Cambrian	14th

1990 – Peugeot Challenge

Peugeot 205 GTI	Panaround	30th
Peugeot 205 GTI	Imber	R
Peugeot 205 GTI	Donington Race	5th
Peugeot 205 GTI	Dukeries	12th
Peugeot 205 GTI	Croft Rallycross	1st
Peugeot 205 GTI	Border	33rd
Peugeot 205 GTI	Zuiderzee Rally	2nd in Class
Peugeot 205 GTI	Flanders	25th
Peugeot 205 GTI	Audi Sport	16th
Peugeot 309 GTI	Great Britain	28th

1991 – Peugeot Challenge

Peugeot 205 GTI	Wyedean	11th
Peugeot 205 GTI	Talkland	R
Peugeot 205 GTI	Ardennes	Class win
Peugeot 205 GTI	Welsh	13th
Peugeot 309 GTI	Mid-Wales Stages	3rd
Peugeot 205 GTI	Dukeries	15th
Peugeot 205 GTI	Kayel Graphics	7th
Subaru Legacy Group N	Border	3rd
Subaru Legacy Group N	Cumbria	R
Peugeot 309 GTI	Manx Int.	14th overall Class win
Peugeot 309 GTI	Audi Sport	11th
Peugeot 309 GTI	Great Britain	16th

R = retired   D = disqualified

1992 - Mintex National Championship

Subaru Legacy Group N	Mazda Winter	2nd
Subaru Legacy Group N	Vauxhall Sport	R
Subaru Legacy Group N	Pirelli	41st
Subaru Legacy Group N	Granite City	8th
Porsche 911	Imber	3rd
Subaru Legacy Group N	Manx Int.	R
Subaru Legacy Group N	Scottish	10th
Subaru Legacy Group N	Severn Valley	1st
Subaru Legacy Group N	Kayel Graphics	2nd
Subaru Legacy Group N	Rally Car Stages	3rd
Peugeot 309 GTI	Elonex	11th
Peugeot 309 GTI	Great Britain	R

1993 – British Championship Subaru

Subaru Legacy Group A	Vauxhall Sport	1st
Subaru Legacy Group A	Pirelli	1st
Subaru Legacy Group A	Scottish	1st
Subaru Legacy Group A	Ulster	R
Subaru Legacy Group A	Manx Int.	1st
Subaru Legacy Group A	Great Britain	7th
Subaru Legacy Group A	Thailand	2nd

1994 – Asia Pacific Championship Subaru

Subaru Impreza Group N	Safari	5th
Subaru Impreza Group A	Indonesia	R
Subaru Impreza Group A	New Zealand	R
Subaru Impreza Group A	Malaysia	2nd
Subaru Impreza Group A	Australia	5th
Subaru Impreza Group A	Hong Kong – Peking	2nd
Subaru Impreza Group A	Great Britain	R
Subaru Impreza Group A	Thailand	2nd

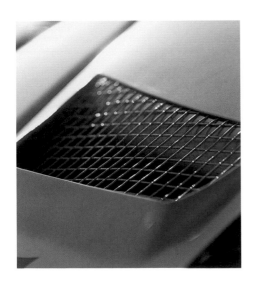

1995 - Subaru

Subaru Impreza Group A	Portugal	7th
Subaru Impreza Group N	Safari	R
Subaru Impreza Group A	New Zealand	R
Subaru Impreza Group A	Hong Kong – Peking	3rd
Subaru Impreza Group A	Great Britain	3rd
Subaru Impreza Group A	Thailand	3rd

1996 – Asia Pacific Championship Mitsubishi

Mitsubishi Lancer Evo III	Thailand	R
Mitsubishi Lancer Evo III	Indonesia	R
Mitsubishi Lancer Evo III	Malaysia	2nd
Mitsubishi Lancer Evo III	Argentina	4th
Mitsubishi Lancer Evo III	New Zealand	1st
Mitsubishi Lancer Evo III	Australia	5th
Mitsubishi Lancer Evo III	Hong Kong – Peking	2nd
Mitsubishi Lancer Evo III	Catalunya	R

1997 - Mitsubishi

Mitsubishi Carisma GT	Safari	2nd
Mitsubishi Carisma GT	Portugal	R
Mitsubishi Carisma GT	Argentina	R
Mitsubishi Carisma GT	Acropolis	4th
Mitsubishi Carisma GT	New Zealand	4th
Mitsubishi Carisma GT	Indonesia	4th
Mitsubishi Carisma GT	Australia	4th
Mitsubishi Carisma GT	Great Britain	4th

1998 – WRC Mitsubishi

Mitsubishi Carisma GT	Monte Carlo	5th
Mitsubishi Carisma GT	Sweden	15th
Mitsubishi Carisma GT	Safari	1st
Mitsubishi Carisma GT	Portugal	4th
Mitsubishi Carisma GT	Catalunya	4th
Mitsubishi Carisma GT	Corsica	R
Mitsubishi Carisma GT	Argentina	4th
Mitsubishi Carisma GT	Acropolis	R
Mitsubishi Carisma GT	New Zealand	9th
Mitsubishi Carisma GT	Finland	5th
Mitsubishi Carisma GT	San Remo	7th
Mitsubishi Carisma GT	Australia	R
Mitsubishi Carisma GT	Great Britain	1st

1999 – WRC Subaru

Subaru Impreza WRC98	Monte Carlo	8th
Subaru Impreza WRC98	Sweden	5th
Subaru Impreza WRC98	Safari	R
Subaru Impreza WRC98	Portugal	4th
Subaru Impreza WRC98	Catalunya	5th
Subaru Impreza WRC99	Corsica	7th
Subaru Impreza WRC99	Argentina	2nd
Subaru Impreza WRC99	Acropolis	1st
Subaru Impreza WRC99	New Zealand	R
Subaru Impreza WRC99	Finland	2nd
Subaru Impreza WRC99	China	2nd
Subaru Impreza WRC99	San Remo	R
Subaru Impreza WRC99	Australia	1st
Subaru Impreza WRC99	Great Britain	1st

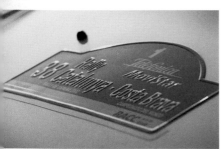

2000 – WRC Subaru

Subaru Impreza WRC99	Monte Carlo	R
Subaru Impreza WRC99	Sweden	4th
Subaru Impreza WRC99	Safari	1st
Subaru Impreza P2000	Portugal	1st
Subaru Impreza P2000	Catalunya	2nd
Subaru Impreza P2000	Argentina	1st
Subaru Impreza P2000	Acropolis	R
Subaru Impreza P2000	New Zealand	R
Subaru Impreza P2000	Finland	R
Subaru Impreza P2000	Cyprus	4th
Subaru Impreza P2000	Corsica	4th
Subaru Impreza P2000	San Remo	R
Subaru Impreza P2000	Australia	2nd
Subaru Impreza P2000	Great Britain	1st

2001 – WRC Subaru

Subaru Impreza WRC2001	Monte Carlo	R
Subaru Impreza WRC2001	Sweden	16th
Subaru Impreza WRC2001	Portugal	4th
Subaru Impreza WRC2001	Catalunya	7th
Subaru Impreza WRC2001	Argentina	2nd
Subaru Impreza WRC2001	Cyprus	2nd
Subaru Impreza WRC2001	Acropolis	R
Subaru Impreza WRC2001	Safari	R
Subaru Impreza WRC2001	Finland	2nd
Subaru Impreza WRC2001	New Zealand	1st
Subaru Impreza WRC2001	San Remo	R
Subaru Impreza WRC2001	Corsica	4th
Subaru Impreza WRC2001	Australia	2nd
Subaru Impreza WRC2001	Great Britain	3rd

2002 – WRC Peugeot

Peugeot 206 WRC	Monte Carlo	8th
Peugeot 206 WRC	Sweden	4th
Peugeot 206 WRC	Corsica	3rd
Peugeot 206 WRC	Catalunya	2nd
Peugeot 206 WRC	Cyprus	2nd
Peugeot 206 WRC	Argentina	D
Peugeot 206 WRC	Acropolis	R
Peugeot 206 WRC	Safari	R

Subaru Impreza WRC2001 Technical Specifications

Engine:	Flat 4-cylinder, 16 valve, turbocharged
Capacity:	1994cc
Bore:	92.0mm
Stroke:	75.0mm
Engine Management:	Subaru programmable electronic engine management system
Power:	300bhp @ 5500rpm
Torque:	48kg-m @ 4000rpm
Transmission:	Prodrive 6-speed electro-hydraulic
	Torque split front/rear: 50/50.
	Electro-hydraulically controlled differentials
Drive System:	4-wheel drive
Suspension:	Front: MacPherson strut
	Rear: MacPherson strut with longitudinal and transverse link
	Brakes: Alcon / Prodrive 305mm ventilated discs and 4-pot calipers front and rear. For asphalt use, front brakes are 366mm ventilated discs with 6-pot water-cooled calipers
Exhaust system:	Ceramic coated, with two, three-way catalytic converters
Steering:	Power assisted rack and pinion
Dimensions:	Overall length: 4405mm
	Overall width: 1770mm
	Overall height: 1390mm
	Wheelbase: 2535mm
	Car weight: 1230kgs (WRC regulation min.)
Data systems:	3 microprocessor controllers; one each for engine, transmission and data-logging, joined by CAN-bus link.
Driver display:	LCD colour monitor with eight selectable data screens
Tyres:	Pirelli
Shock Absorbers:	Bilstein / Prodrive, fully adjustable with remote reservoirs.
Radio Equipment:	Kenwood
Turbo Charger:	IHI - with WRC regulation 34mm restrictor
Spark Plugs:	NGK
Wheels:	OZ magnesium
Fuel Tank capacity:	80 litres

Peugeot 205 WRC2002 Technical Specifications

Engine:	Type: XU9J4
Installation:	Front-mounted, transversely
Number of cylinders:	4
Capacity:	1997 cc
Bore x stroke:	85 x 88 mm
Max power:	300 bhp at 5250 rpm
Max torque:	535 Nm at 3500 rpm
Head:	aluminium
Valves:	4 per cylinder
Cylinder block:	aluminium
	Double overhead camshaft
Engine management:	Magnetti Marelli Step 9
Turbocharger:	Garret Allied Signal
Lubrication:	via carbon wet sump
Transmission :	
Clutch:	three-plate AP carbon, 5 or 6-inch
Gearbox:	Xtrac 6-speed sequential, longitudinally mounted
Differentials:	front and central diffs are electronically controlled
Suspension :	
Front:	pseudo MacPherson
Rear:	pseudo MacPherson
Shock absorbers:	Peugeot
Steering :	Rack and pinion, power assisted
Brakes :	Front: 355 mm ventilated discs, 6-piston calipers
	Rear: 330 mm ventilated discs, 6-piston calipers
Tyres :	Michelin
Dimensions :	
Wheelbase:	2.468 m
Length:	4.005 m
Width:	1.770 m
Weight:	1230 kg
Fuel tank capacity:	85 litres

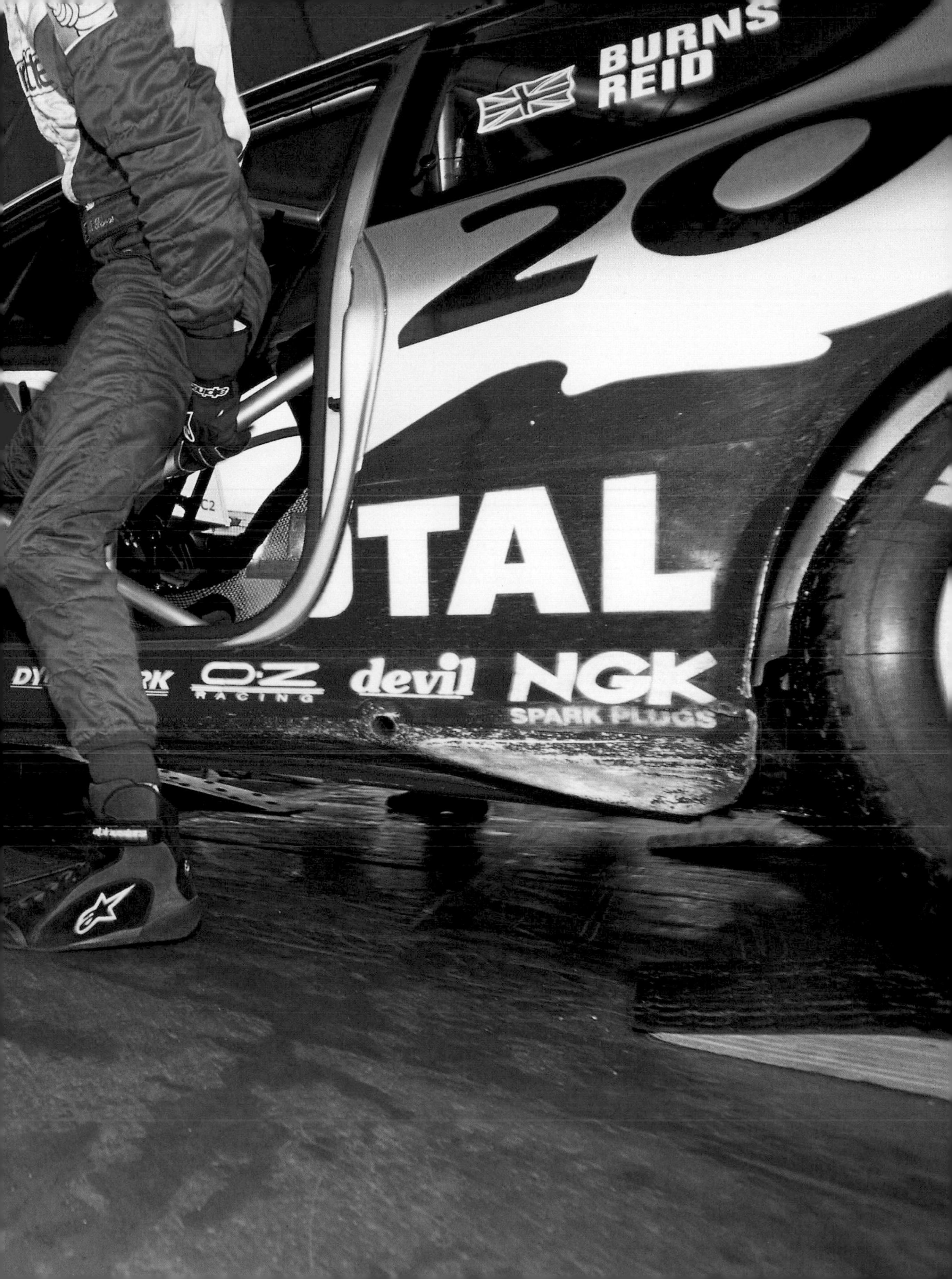
BURNS
REID
20
TAL
O·Z
RACING
devil
NGK
SPARK PLUGS

Acknowledgements

Special thanks go to the following for making sure that I actually had something to write about:

Zöe - for her patience, unselfishness and the faith she has in me.

Dad - Alex, who gave me so much time and dedication during my teenage years. I can only hope that what I do now gives him as much pleasure as he gave me then.

Mum - Denise, who never once told me to get a proper job.

Jo Burns - thanks for joining me just when it got tough.

David Williams - for his generosity, vision and friendship. I would never have achieved what I have without him.

Robert Reid - for his ceaseless preparation and dedication.

The recce, test, rally and human performance team at Prodrive - for the hours and hours of work it takes to win.

Robbie Head and Steve Turvey - for the past four years my eyes on the road before I see it.

Clare Caudwell - who in the last four years has coped with me and my ways.

There are so many people who have helped me over the past 20 years, it would be an insult to miss out any of them by printing a list here. All I can say is that I appreciate their efforts enormously because I can now recognize the one thing they all gave me - their time.

And finally...

thanks to Jon and Sandra for providing the direction and enthusiasm for making *Driving Ambition* work.

Rupert Lancaster and Sheila Crowley at my publishers Hodder & Stoughton and designer Ned Hoste: thanks for all the skill and hard work in bringing this book into existence.

Peter J Fox - who specialises in wildlife photography - a perfect choice for this book. Thanks for the imagination and skill that is demonstrated quite clearly on these pages.

Colin McMaster and the McKlein agency - without doubt the finest photographers in world rallying. I am proud and honoured to display so much previously unpublished work of theirs in my book.

Picture Acknowledgements

All the photographs in this book were taken either by Peter Fox or the McKlein Agency, except for pictures from the early part of my career. Thanks to David Williams for supplying some of those and to the following for permission to reproduce them: Nick Ford, Speedsports (Ruthin), Tony Large Photographic, Guardian Newspapers Limited.

Text copyright © 2002
by Richard Burns
Photography © 2002 by Peter Fox and McKlein

First published in Great Britain in 2002 by
Hodder and Stoughton
A division of Hodder Headline

A Hodder & Stoughton book

1 3 5 7 9 10 8 6 4 2

A CIP catalogue record for this title is available
from the British Library

ISBN 0 340 82517 0

Typeset in Frutiger Light
Printed and bound in Great Britain by Butler &
Tanner, Frome, Somerset

Designed by Ned Hoste/2h

Hodder and Stoughton
A division of Hodder Headline
338 Euston Road
London NW1 3BH